D0982897

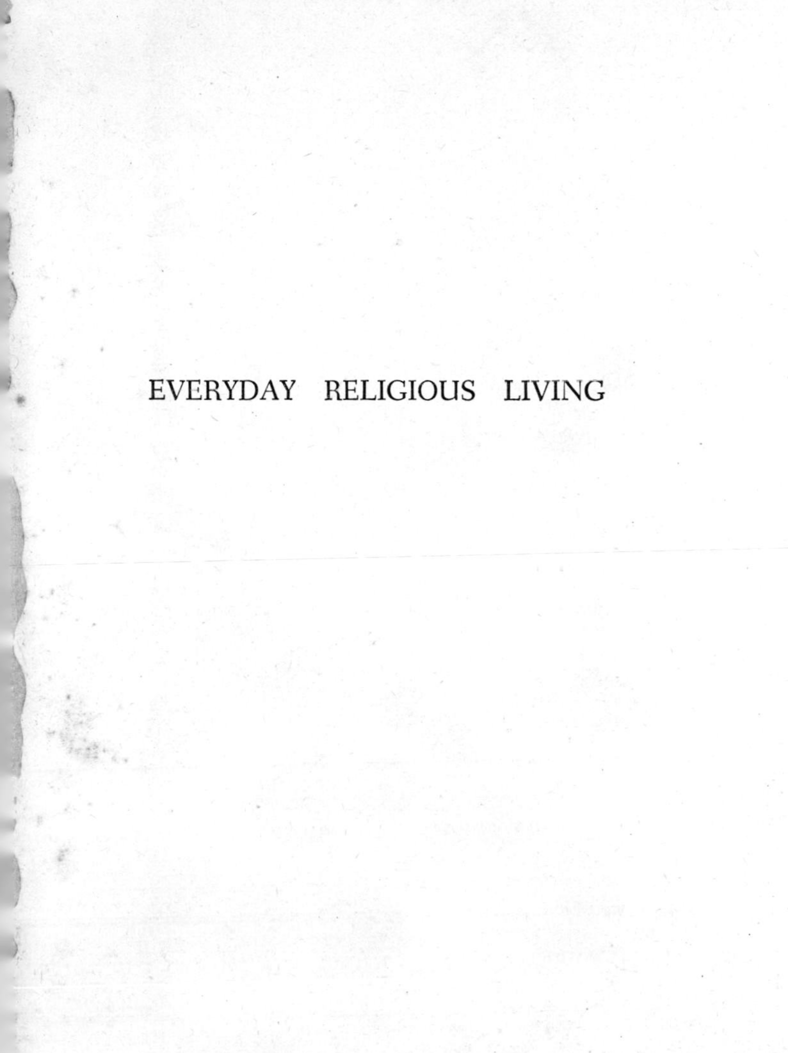

EVERYDAY RELIGIOUS LIVING

Everyday
RELIGIOUS LIVING

JOSEPH FORT NEWTON

New York *Nashville*
ABINGDON-COKESBURY PRESS

EVERYDAY RELIGIOUS LIVING

Library of Congress Catalog Card Number: 51-14229

B

SET UP, PRINTED, AND BOUND BY THE PARTHENON PRESS, AT NASHVILLE, TENNESSEE, UNITED STATES OF AMERICA

FOREWORD

When Joseph Fort Newton died on January 24, 1950, the galley proofs of his eighty-third book were spread out on his desk, all but the last few sheets turned over to show they had been read. In due time this book came from the press and proved to be one of the most popular of the eighty-three. It was called *Everyday Religion,* and it contained sixty-five brief messages—conversations, one might almost call them—that applied the truth in some verse of scripture to the problems and opportunities we all face day by day.

Post cards inviting comments were included in many of the copies, and large numbers of these came in with words of appreciation. Not a few asked whether more of these conversational messages were available. Fortunately the answer was "Yes." Over several years Dr. Newton had written a weekly column in the *Philadelphia Evening Bulletin,* called "The Saturday Sermon." He had made up the book *Everyday Religion* by selecting columns that had stimulated people to write to him. As he said in the Foreword, "This book was suggested by my readers, who have selected nearly every sermon in it, and many more—too many to include."

From the "many more," then, it was easy, with the help of Mrs. Newton and Harrison W. Fry, religious editor of the *Bulletin,* to choose another sixty-five for a new book.

EVERYDAY RELIGIOUS LIVING is thus another volume of *Everyday Religion,* but it would be misleading to call it a "second" volume, for each stands alone, and either can be read first. So the newer book rather is called by a separate title that is really the same thing in other words. To Dr. Newton, as any reader will quickly recognize, "religion" meant "religious living." In fact, for the most part it meant "everyday religious living." And so it comes that one can read one of these messages in the morning and expect to find an opportunity to apply its truth before the day ends. This was the sort of religion that Dr. Newton believed and practiced and preached—a religion that turns divine truth into strength and vision and sympathy and aspiration for the needs of every day.

THE PUBLISHERS

CONTENTS

WHAT IS LIFE FOR?

"That they might have life . . . more abundantly." John 10:10

WHAT IS life for? To live, of course. Yet how few do much with life, or make anything out of it. Some are living, others only partly living. There are too many unsmiling faces, too many eyes that are lusterless.

Too many feet merely shuffle into the future, without hope or joy. Others are seamed by sickness, broken by burdens, drained by discouragement and defeat. Rarely do we meet a person radiantly and vividly alive.

To be sure, there are certain basic human wishes which all of us share, young as well as old, men as well as women, the denial of which makes us unhappy. If those wishes find fulfillment, we are happy; if not, we are unhappy.

We desire recognition from others—we want to know that we count, and count for something, and that what we do is worth while. In short, we want to "belong," else we feel not only shut out, but lonely and useless.

By the same fact, we desire affectionate response from our fellows—someone to love and be loved by. If this deep desire is thwarted, we may seek emotional substitutes elsewhere, often in ways devious and dangerous.

Also, we desire some measure of security and a sense of at-homeness in our situation. If this is lacking, we are driven every which way, distracted. Economic insecurity is bad enough, but emotional insecurity is even worse.

Finally, we desire experiences that are fresh and vital and vivid enough to rescue us from stagnation and boredom. Hence our hobbies, sports, travel, art interests, all the many ways we seek to divert ourselves from the grind.

Human beings hate drabness, even more than danger. They will do almost anything to avoid being bored, to escape full routine, to free themselves from going round and round without getting anywhere, like a squirrel in a cage.

To sum it up, we desire physical fulfillment—food, clothing, home, health, social satisfaction. We want personal development—knowledge, training, skill; we want to be citizens of the world and of the ages by education. Of course we want the joy of comradeship, contacts intimate, warm, personal. We cannot live without love, sympathy, loyalty. We want above all things the joy of creative work, making beautiful things, doing work that counts.

All these basic desires, each honorable after its kind, are selfish, and in seeking their satisfaction we can be selfish. In the beginning of life selfishness is necessary, but if it continues, life is ruined.

How many times one has seen people have the fulfillment of all these wishes—recognition, even fame, troops of friends, culture, security, rich and varied experiences, and yet make little or nothing out of life. What wastage!

If we want recognition, we must do something to win it. Even if we do something worth while, we do not always get credit for it. But if it is good work, it is its own reward, even if the world disregards it or forgets it.

Against the wishes of her family and friends, Florence Nightingale dared to do what no woman had ever done—nurse wounded men in war. She won little recognition until she was too wise to need it, and too old to enjoy it.

In the same way, if we would have friends, we must be friendly. Instead of building walls around ourselves, we must build bridges into other lives. By as much as we get out of ourselves, and get ourselves off our hands, by so much we are happy.

As for security, no one has very much of it in the world today. Too much security weakens us, too little may destroy us. Of one thing we may be sure: in the days ahead of us no one will have much security unless there is more security for all.

Our deepest need is for inner, emotional security, and a simple religious faith is the secret of it. "Thou wilt keep him in perfect peace, whose mind is stayed on thee: because he trusteth in thee." Even in wild and whirling days, when nothing is certain but uncertainty, the House of Peace is open to us.

Whether we shall have a rich and varied experience, all depends on how many facets we have to our personality and how many interests we have in life. If we twang away on one string, the music of life will be dull and unexciting.

President Eliot of Harvard used to say that 90 per cent of his work was routine. But he was willing to have it so, for the sake of the other 10 per cent of opportunity to do creative work, new and full of adventure.

It all depends on our attitude toward life, whether we by-pass it or let it pass by us. Keats, Burns, and Shelley died before forty, but they lived more in a few years than most of us would live in a century—lived more, suffered more.

Jesus came, he said, that we might have life more abundantly. He had little or no money, he had no social position, and more enemies than friends. Yet "on a shoe-string," as we say, he lived more and did more than anyone who ever lived.

The swift and awful gift of life is for each of us. What we do with it, how we use it, is up to us. We can live "more abundantly" if we try.

DEEP LIVING

"Turn back, dwell deep." Jer. 49:8

"CAPTAIN, I suppose you know every sandbank in the river," said a passenger on a Mississippi steamboat in the old days.

"No, I don't," said the captain, who had learned a lot of wisdom from Old Man River. "It would be a waste of time," he added.

"What! A waste of time?" exclaimed the passenger. "If you don't know where the sandbanks are, how can you pilot the boat?"

"Yes, a waste of time," the captain repeated. "Why should I go kicking about among the sandbanks? I know where the deep waters are."

A whole philosophy of life was in his reply, whether we run a steamboat or try to pilot our lives through the years. Also, it may show why we are in "shallows and miseries," always getting stuck in the mud.

It is a waste of time to be bumping into all the sandbanks in the river of life—unless we were sent to survey the stream, discover the sandbanks, and find the way to go. But that has been done many times before.

Let us be honest with ourselves—we are in trouble either because we do not know where the deep water is, or we are afraid to take the risk! Unless we have the courage to live deeply, even dangerously, we can hardly live at all.

Shallow living is dangerous too, far more than we realize.

"Launch out into the deep," Jesus told his disciples long ago. In spite of the whirling, swirling currents, we are safer in deep waters which move quietly, sweeping us to our destination. We must take the risks of life, the risks of faith, the risks of love, else we die without having lived at all.

It is far more dangerous to flounder in the shallows than to brave the depths, where life finds its true fulfillment. Why bump the sandbanks and be a stick-in-the-mud, when life was meant for adventure and deep soundings?

The prophet Jeremiah lived in a wild and stormy age. Fear was in the air, disaster hung upon every horizon. North, east, south, west, everywhere it was dark, as it has been in our age, and still is. The thudding hoofs of savage horsemen echoed in his ears; the shadows of Assyria blackened the sky.

What did he tell his people to do? "Flee ye, turn back, dwell deep," that is, seek safety by dwelling far back in the hills. Just so today, in the midst of threats and instabilities, calm and wise souls will seek security in the depths below the surface, in "the deepest thing in all nature."

A friend tells how he met a lovely English girl who had been born and lived all her life on an island off the coast of South America. It was there he met her. She was all excited because it had been decided only a week before that she was to go "back home" to England.

"Back home?" he asked. "How can you go back home?

You were born here. Brought up here. This is your home." She shook her head. Although she had been born and raised in a faraway place, she said, "No, England is my home." She was living deeply, obeying something in her very blood and bone.

The seagirt island, steeped in history, ivied with legend; its gray mists, its lovely lanes, its old cathedrals, "hymns to God in soaring stone," Oxford, Glastonbury, "saints and cream and Devon things," all these and much else for which no words exist—England lived in the depths of her soul.

One thinks of that scene in the Bible when the people redug "the wells of salvation," long sanded up. Surface water would not do; in fact, did not exist in the desert. Something like that is going on among us. In the long-lived storm of great events we are renewing our interest in religion—in the things which neither time nor death can touch or take away.

A shallow, surface, vivacious life fails us. "Hollow men," T. S. Eliot described people after World War I, empty, having no rich inwardness. It was true. One spoke of the things of the spirit, and people stared at the preacher, puzzled. Instead, they sought all kinds of spiritual gadgets, trying to find some kind of reality by the turn of a trick, there were cults no end.

No, superficial living does not satisfy; we must dig deep, dwell deep, if we are to be fortified and sustained amid the whirl of events. Everything moves swiftly today, but some things do not grow old, do not go out of date. To learn to live for things eternal is "to make our lives eternal," as Dante told us.

All saints, seers, and mystics tell us this truth. "The eternal God is thy refuge, and underneath are the everlasting arms," said Moses, old, stricken, and about to die. The ninetieth psalm tells the same august truth, also the ninety-first, "He that dwelleth in the secret place of the Most High shall abide under the shadow of the Almighty." This is not pious talk; it is the first truth and the last.

As Julia Ward Howe said of old age, "Do not fear age, the sugar of life is at the bottom of the cup." If we learn how to live with God, live in him, we shall find in him, and in our own souls, that which will make us victors over anything that life or death can do to us. "Dwell deep!"

THE SACRAMENT OF SERVICE

"I am among you as he that serveth." Luke 22:27

HERE IS the secret of the greatest life ever lived upon the earth. It was the life that interprets life, showing what our fleeting days can be when they are free from grasping greed and sordid self-seeking.

No wonder it makes us wistful just to think about it. Jesus came, he said, not to be ministered to, but to minister. To do good to others, not to have things done for him. It was an utterly self-spending life.

Without any of the things that we think necessary to life—without money, or very little, without office or rank or social power—he did more for humanity in a few short and busy years than anyone who ever lived.

Some men live to get. Life to them is a system of self-service. The words of Jesus, "It is more blessed to give than to receive," have no meaning for them. For them life is measured by what they gain.

Others live to give—life is not ingrowing, but outgrowing. They give themselves, forgive others, and live with thanksgiving. They alone know such happiness as we may hope to find and know amid our fleeting mortal days.

The men and women whom we remember and revere, whose names shine like stars, did not take life for granted, but for gratitude. They gave their utmost to the highest, pouring out their time and strength for others.

Service is the great sacrament—that is, "an outward and visible sign of an inward and spiritual grace." A cup of cool water given in the name of love, a kindness done in return for unkindness—these are the greatest things on earth.

Such is the strategy of doing good. It disarms its enemies by its self-forgetful lovingkindness. It softens hearts not turned to stone; it awakens faiths and feelings in human beings, of which they had been unaware.

What kind of service is sacramental? Any kind that helps to lift the load on the backs and hearts of our fellow souls. The humblest ministry, no less than the highest, takes on haunting meanings when done in love.

Hear now the words of Browning, a goldenhearted poet, "All service ranks the same with God." There is no high, no low; it is not what we do, but how we do it, with what faith and motive, with what spirit and healing skill.

A bishop, a baker, a candlestick maker, a wife washing dishes, a man digging a ditch, a preacher in his pulpit, a farmer plowing a field, Brother Lawrence with his pots and pans, equally with a poet with his lyrics—all serve.

Many kinds of life must be lived, many sorts of work must be done—some of it hard work, heavy work. Yet no matter what we do, whether it is writing music or making a road, "all service ranks the same with God."

Three hundred years ago George Herbert lived in the village of Bemerton, England, but only for a few years, when he fell victim of the great white plague. He wrote a little book of poems called *The Temple,* and then died. When a book lives for three centuries, it has something eternal in it. One stanza of his book tells us a truth which we need to know and lay to heart:

> Who sweeps a room, as for Thy laws,
> Makes that and th' action fine.

Such a faith and spirit turn drudgery into happy labor. It makes our work not just a job, but a joy; a task, however trying, is lifted up and given meaning when it is done for something, or Someone, greater than ourselves.

An old and wise story tells of two men cutting stone. The work was hard and the sun was hot. A passer-by asked one man what he was doing. "Look and see for yourself; I am cutting a stone," was the rather curt reply.

Not far away he asked the other man the same question, and he said, with a gleam in his eye, "Sir, I am building a cathedral." One saw his work as merely a job all by itself, a thing to get done and have done with it. The other man saw the same work as it was related to a vast design, as having a place in a pattern, the working out of which would make a house of God. He felt it an honor to have a part in such a dream.

To know that our work, whatever it may be, has a place and part in the vast network of human service not only makes our labor lighter, but lifts it up and gives it meaning—we see its value in a larger context.

It makes us feel that we are not alone, doing a hard job all by itself, for the pay we get and nothing more. It gives dignity to even the humblest work to see it in its true meaning, as an act, a sacrament, of service.

We are here on earth to make a living and to make a life. Sometimes the two may be the same, but not always. Each must make his keep, pull his weight—make enough and to spare, in order to share with others who lack.

But our chief duty and reason for our being is to make a life, make it clean and valiant, heroic and humble, faithful and fruitful, and so leave the world a little better than we found it—our service a sacrament of God.

LET US LIVE WHILE WE ARE ALIVE

"Be not therefore anxious for the morrow."
Matt. 6:34 (A.S.V.)

In the King James Version the text reads, "Take therefore no thought for the morrow." But Jesus did not mean it that way. It would preclude making any plan for the future, for ourselves or others, or carrying out any purpose.

No, he meant fretful, futile anxiety, foreboding—worry. Alas, man is born to worry as the sparks fly upward. All of us are experts at it because we practice it so much. If we have nothing to worry about, we make up something.

Some people have a worrying temperament. L. P. Jacks, the English philosopher, preacher, and story writer, wrote his autobiography at eighty. He tells us that he cannot recall an hour in his life, even as a child, when he was free from anxiety, due to uncertainty about what would happen next.

But temperament can be modified, as I can testify. If my own temperament had had its way, I would have lived in a dun-colored world, under a sky as gray as a tired face. Happily, a sense of God rescued me from that dismal fate.

During World War II a man—as good a man as ever stood in shoes—said to me, "I think I am losing my mind; I'm so worried about the war." He would have been losing his mind, or else been an utter moron, if he had not been anxious when the fate of liberty, justice, and mercy hung in the balance!

But anxiety, if it is not checked, will eat away our very souls. Hawthorne, our great novelist, was so horrified by the Civil War—its dark news, and darker imaginings—that he crept away to die, brokenhearted.

Anxiety, to put the point plainly, can be destructive, as we know well enough. But it can also be creative. Jesus did not come into the world to give us soothing sirup, or "a ghastly smooth life, dead of soul." Never!

"Think not that I am come to send peace on earth: I came not to send peace, but a sword." He knew that it was only through creative anxiety of the highest sort that his kingdom could be built. Perhaps "concern" is the right word, in the sense in which the people of the Society of Friends use the word.

But chronic, unbelieving, fear-ridden anxiety is a habit, a force, which not only weakens our morale, but can easily destroy our usefulness, or even life itself. We must flee this state of mind as we would flee a plague.

Worry is the right word for it—fitful, fretful, faithless, fruitless worry, which wears us down and unfits us for any useful thought or work. Worry is when we think not with our minds but with our emotions. We let our feelings—our fears, chiefly—tease, tear, and harass us.

Or more often our imagination takes the wheel and goes for a joy ride. We pop awake at night in a cold sweat, and the imagination puts on a show, a drama of the thing we fear, and makes us see it again and again.

No wonder we are worn out, unfit for the day and its task. Lack of emotional control is devastating. As someone has said, in a jungle one may worry about snakes, but if he looks for them under the carpet, he is a neurotic.

The question is whether we shall handle our emotions, or let them mishandle us. If we cannot master our emotions, we need help and we can get it. Men of science and men of the spirit can aid us with new skills of habit craft.

Here our religion is our best friend. "Thou wilt keep him in perfect peace, whose mind is stayed on thee: because he trusteth in thee." These are not merely pious words; they show us the way to a sanctuary of serenity.

Faith is the best armor against wasting worry—faith in God, faith in life, faith in that in our own soul which can make us masters of life, not victims of it. Life is tense today, but it need not tear us to pieces.

A natural "concern" in face of difficulty or danger is wholesome. Life can be hard, terribly hard and full of hazard. It was meant to be so; otherwise we would be a race of softies. Also, its moods are as many as its jolts.

Lincoln had moods of blue-black melancholy, as if he were mourning over some grief that never in time or eternity could be healed. Yet despite his dark moods, he did more for his race than any "glad-handed" man.

In short, Lincoln made the best of his moods; he did not let them make the worst of him. They were a family trait, known as "the Lincoln horrors," Carl Sandburg tells us. But he did not use that fact as an alibi, as so many do.

"Look up, not down; look out, not within, and lend a hand," was the wise saying of a greatly beloved preacher years ago. If we find ourselves turning inward, brooding and lonely, we must open the window, go to see someone, give someone a lift.

Our night thoughts are the biggest liars on earth. They always stretch things beyond reason and belief. They will make us morbid before we know it, unless we have a care. Fatigue explains half our inner troubles.

Life was not meant to be fear-haunted and worry-worn. It is too wonderful—just being alive in this amazing world. Why spoil it by regrets for the past, or forebodings for the future? Let us live while we are alive.

FROM DEATH UNTO LIFE

"We know that we have passed from death unto life, because we love." I John 3:14

THESE WORDS reverse the usual order of things. We do not pass from life unto death, not from dust unto dust, but from death unto life—life triumphant, regnant, spreading its wings for flight.

Such words, if read in the lucid interval between Easter Day and the Ascension, are luminous. They answer the questions which are in our hearts when we think of our own exodus from the earth, and still more when we try to follow in imagination those who vanish from us.

Jesus did not answer questions directly; he did something better and wiser. He taught—nay, he revealed—the triumph of personality, but he left the details of the afterlife in discreet silence, lest they interfere with the life that now is. He confirmed faith without satisfying curiosity.

Must we admit, then, that we know nothing at all about life after death, and that we are left in a world of dim hints and cryptic analogies, with no glad assurance? Far, very far from it! We know much, very much, about life after death, both as to its realities and its conditions; all, in fact, that we need to know, if we are wise enough to lay the facts to heart.

Now take thought. All the realities that make life great, deep, and rewarding, giving it meaning here and value hereafter, abide untouched by time and death. They are both realities and prophecies, and if we ponder them deeply, they light up the future, while they bless and guide us here.

Just consider. God lives here, hereafter, and unto everlasting; "in him we live, and move, and have our being." In him there is no death, no darkness, no distance. Pray, what more do we want or need to know? To know God, Jesus told us, is life eternal—"all live unto him!"

Without God, in whose great hand we stand, life would be a horror and a death; not a destiny, but a doom. God lives, and he is the home of all souls, here and forever, "our dwelling place in all generations." We cannot go where God is not; the sky begins at the top of the ground.

In the old Bible we are taught that man lives in God; in the New Testament we learn that God lives in man. If we learn to live in God, for God, unto God, not for our petty selves and our puny ends, then we live the eternal life in time. Otherwise we have no real life anywhere.

By the same token, if we let God live in us, let him use our little lives for his ends, as for his will, then we really live, and what we call death is but a cloud shadow. The eternal life is not a dim state into which we enter at death; it is a present reality and prophecy.

Add now the truth of the continuity of life, as Jesus taught it. "Today shalt thou be with me in paradise"—that is, a garden—he said to the man who died with him. Today, before the sun goes down; we know each other here, we shall know each other there—no spiritual law is clouded. Truth, love, goodness abide, untouched by death.

The ordeal of physical death may be profound, but no moral truth, no spiritual reality, is lost or obscured by it. Life is unbroken; there is no gap or gulf separating life here from life farther on. Nor is there any redemption, here or anywhere, until we learn to do justly, to love mercy, and to live humbly with God. What more do we ask to know?

How and where do we live after death? To our imagination life beyond time may seem like a bare, blank void, but that is only seeming. No one of us could have imagined the conditions of this life before we entered it. How could Shakespeare eat mutton and think the thoughts of Hamlet? It is a mystery past finding out—but it was a fact.

To limit moral progress to our life on earth is to stereotype humanity in eternal imperfection. Death does not make a man a saint, although it touches the lowliest with majesty. Nor does it petrify us in sin. It may even set us free from handicaps which beset us here. No man may hope to be saved until he is better than the best man knows himself to be.

God is love, else he is not God. By as much as love—not as a soft sentiment, but as a law and principle of being—by so much do we live here and hereafter. Because God is love, he is known only by love; and to love him and our fellow souls is to defeat death with life.

Some of us hold, with the great and simple Lincoln, that in the long last it will be "all or none." The love of God—

the mightiest and gentlest force in the universe—will not, cannot, let any soul go. Who can defeat a love that "beareth all things, . . . endureth all things"?

The love of God is the first truth and the last, and our eternal hope.

MADE OVER AGAIN

"Ye must be born again." John 3:7

Two FRIENDS talked through the night about the things of the spirit.

"Except a man be born again, he cannot see the kingdom of God," said the young Teacher, setting forth a truth as deep as life itself.

To the literal mind of Nicodemus the words of the Teacher were a riddle. "How can a man be born when he is old?" he asked. To him, as to many men, certain things were impossible. As if human nature were like cement—once set it can never be changed.

The Teacher was patient but firm. He was speaking of the birth of the spirit, which is like the blowing of the wind. It blows where it wills; we hear the sound thereof, but the source is secret. So the soul of man is reborn again and again, touched and awakened by invisible influences.

Yes, human nature can be changed, if not in its faculties and driver, then in its spirit and goal. In New Zealand as late as 1845, cannibals were changed to Christians in twenty years. It is not necessary to get away from human nature, but to alter its inner attitude of mind and heart.

Our human life, if we see it aright, is a series of rebirths. Each of the "seven ages of man" is a rebirth, a new start on a higher level. The road of life is not a smooth slope but a rough journey, in which we leap from one level to the next. The awakening and unfolding of the soul is a romance.

One watches the wonder of it in the growth of a child. Self is the first center of life. A baby is utterly selfish, and must be to survive. His life thereafter, if he is healthy, is getting away from himself, getting out of himself into the lives of others. If he grows, he is born many times.

Otherwise he becomes a concentration camp in himself, all intake and no outgo. Our basic defect—if not the root of all evil, certainly the source of most of it—is self-centeredness; life ingrowing, not outgoing. Our real birthday is when we get away from the idea that life is getting, not giving.

Often this awakening is sudden, in the light of a flash. Sometimes it comes slowly, by gradual growth. Some of the noblest souls can name no day or date of their rebirth. No matter; just so they discover that life is not a cafeteria for their own self-service, but is a chance to serve their fellows. Just so they get themselves off their hands—then life really begins.

What we need, all of us, is to have the center of gravity shifted in us from self-seeking to self-spending. In religion it is called "conversion," a turning about, being born again. Alas, few of us are converted often enough, deeply enough, far enough; we are converted only in spots.

Too many of us are pious in some ways, and pagan in other ways—sermon-saturated pagans. One may be selfish even in religion, forgetting that Jesus said that if a man seeks to save his soul, he loses it. In any case, religion is not a scramble for safety; it is faith, hope, and love.

Fear of God may be "the beginning of wisdom," but to be afraid of God is the death of religion. "Fear not," was a favorite byword of Jesus. As if he had said, "There is nothing to be afraid of but fear itself. Love God, trust him; religion is love, because God is love. Lift up your hearts!"

At two o'clock Good Friday morning in 1852, John Ruskin, thirty-three years of age, began thinking about his past life. It had been a clean life, devoted to art, but he was disgusted with it, because, he said, "I saw that I had been working for myself in one way or another. This will never do."

Of course two o'clock in the morning is an awful time to think about anything, but he faced up to the facts of his life without flinching. He found that he had no joy in his past life, no hope of another life. He was as miserable as a man can be, bogged down in self-disgust.

"So, after thinking, I resolved that if I would act as if the Bible were true, I would believe in Christ and take him as my Master in whatever I did. When I arose in the morning, I felt a peace and a spirit in me that I had never known before." Truly, he was born again into a new life.

Yet years later, there came a black time, when he lost faith in the immortal life. It was a bitter day, dark, lonely, hopeless. But by the mercy of God, the cloud lifted, and there was clear shining. He was born again, and walked thereafter under lifting skies until the falling daylight.

How often we need to be taken to pieces and put together again, born again, not once but many times in the upward advance of the soul. He is wise who, like Ruskin, calmly faces his own soul and makes a clean decision, as a deliberate choice, not as a last, desperate, fear-driven resort.

We must be "born again," and again, and again, before we are born into the immortal life.

HAPPY NEW YEAR!

"The days of our years." Ps. 90:10

We all wish one another "A Happy New Year!" How can we make it so? It will be a new year if we meet it with faith, without fear, facing all that it brings, making the best of everything, and not letting anything make the worst of us. Not what happens to us but what happens in us—that is what counts.

Such truths are trite, like the truth that two and two make four, or that selfishness defeats itself. If we have to live in a world, we do not have to let the world live in us. Else we are sure to be all tangled up, half slave and half free, torn by strife and terrified by threats and nameless fears.

Our human life moves on two levels—a surface level where culture, civilization, statecraft, applied science, labor, the fixing of the value of money, concern us deeply. On this level we do our work well or ill, buy, sell, and get gain; we are alert, active, eager, and the days are two few and too short.

Then there is a deeper level of life, a subsoil, so to name it, which remains much the same, amid many chances and changes on the surface. Even our religion, if it moves only on the first level, is apt to lose its religious quality and become a thing of social reform, as it did with most of the prophets.

On the deeper level of life things remain much the same,

whatever takes place on the surface. There birth and death, love and play, the secret sources of strength, the inner confidences, hope, faith, and dreams are the real things. The book of Job and the words of Jesus speak to that deeper life.

What we are in our deeper life decides what we do with the days as they come and go, whether many or few. If we have won inner peace, deep down where our real life is, storms do not shake us, sorrows do not crush us, time has no tyranny over us. "As he thinketh in his heart," so is a man, the Bible tells us.

One can begin so many things with a new year, as with a new friend. Unless we are better than the best man knows himself to be, each of us needs a going over, a checkup. Some habits need to be dropped and better ones formed. Else we may lose our real and deeper life from living too much on the surface.

Otherwise we may find it hard to live with ourselves, much less with others, before we know it. It is time to take ourselves in hand a bit, tighten loose belts, stop knocks, and make ourselves physically, mentally, and spiritually fit. A little self-attention will work wonders if taken in time.

Many a "heart condition" is brought on by neglect of those inner arts by which we learn poise without passion, weariness without worry, serenity without sloth, lightness without levity—how to work without strain and to rest without idling. Then we are using our religion as a steering wheel, not as a spare tire.

Morley, in trying to explain how Gladstone kept such amazing vitality, and stood on tiptoe until nearly ninety, could only say, "He lived from a greater depth." So he did, offering his morning prayer, or making his Communion, in the chapel on his estate before taking his train for London.

"Put habit on the side of the inner life," he wrote to his children. The more spiritual attitudes we make habitual in our hearts, the more sure we are to stand erect when ill winds blow. *The Practice of the Presence of God* is not merely the title of a classic little book; it can be done any time, anywhere.

What are we going to do with the new year? Add another year to our lives, or add a new life to a new year? Some people move back into the past, settle down and live there —walking into the future backward. Like old soldiers I used to hear talk as a boy, forever fighting old battles over again.

Others live only for today, its duty and task, its hurry and flurry; when it is ended, they drop it in the wastebasket. Eat, drink, and be merry, live while you are alive, it will all be over soon enough. There is a sense in which we ought to drop a day when it is done, but not drop it out of its context.

Still others are victims of the future. They overload it, putting forward into tomorrow, or next week, things that belong to today, or yesterday, until the future becomes a lumber room piled too high ever to climb over—as our attics often are. How astonished we are when we visit them at what we find.

If we are to make the new year really new, we must learn to be victors over time, not victims of it. We must have the energy and art to make something beautiful of it, or it will make something ugly of us. How often we see people after a long time and wonder what time has done to them—some faces exquisitely carved, some cold, hard, with lines of cynicism or sadness.

"The days of our years are threescore years and ten." Yet so often they fly away. Let us trust God, who knows nothing of time, but whose mercy endures forever; let us live every day given us as a gem out of eternity; and let us be a little kinder than necessary, every day, to everybody. May the new year be a short year, since sorrows make the days so slow; may it be a year full of all the best things. Happy New Year!

FAITH FOR LIVING

"Thy faith hath saved thee." Luke 7:50

ALL OF us live by faith all the time. We never take a train, start a business, get married, or make a friend, save as an act of faith.

Faith is one of the greatest forces of life. It is in our human world what electricity is in the physical world. A tiny grain of faith, said Jesus, can remove mountains into the sea—and it is true.

It is faith that finds facts and the meaning of facts. We must have faith in order to know, and on the basis of what we know we raise to higher faith. What we know was once a matter of faith. Franklin had faith that electricity could be put to work; he flew his kite and found the facts.

Jesus believed that love is the law of life. He acted upon his faith, and proved it. Faith is not believing things in spite of the evidence; it is doing things in spite of difficulty. It is the courage to act upon an insight, and the quiet patience to follow up and work out what we trust to be true.

"Not truth, but faith it is that keeps the world alive," a wise poet tells us. Faith is dynamic power like radium—not our power, but power in us flowing through us. As our bodies are built up out of solar energy in the form of food, so our lives are made vibrant, meaningful, and useful by power which we receive from the source of being—a power not our own.

In her lovely book *Let Us Have Faith* Helen Keller put it simply, "Faith is not a cushion for me to fall back upon; it is my working energy." By the power of faith she overcame her appalling handicap—deafness, dumbness, blindness—as we can overcome anything that life or death can do to us.

Enemy Number 1 in life is fear. It takes a million forms, makes us a race of creepers. Faith is the one thing working against it. When fear knocks at the door and faith opens it, there is no one there! When faith fades for any reason, or none, fear crawls into the heart—a vile and slimy thing.

Faith is the life principle; fear is the death principle. Faith is the plus quality; fear is the minus quality. Faith releases power; fear inhibits it, closes all doors and makes us prisoners. How many people live—if it can be called living—as slaves of fear, down in a dark dungeon!

When Jesus said to the sinful woman, "They faith hath saved thee," she must have been surprised, if not doubtful. She thought he did it, lifting a load of guilt from her heart. Often he said the same thing to people he healed of physical ills—he healed them, but he forgave them too.

How do we get faith? We do not have to get it. We have it already, or the capacity for it, only we are afraid to use it. We are born with faith, or the faculty for it, just as we are born with our head, heart, and hands. Today, alas, we have secured a complex; we are afraid to take risks.

Yet all the while we have the capacity to receive power—

not our own power, but power which will pour into us when we are ready and willing to receive it. We need power for living, power to overcome obsessions, frustrations, handicaps, and fears. We are weak when we need to be strong, and faith will make us strong.

The power of God is available to every soul, everywhere. "Obey the law of the power and the power will obey you," is a wise and true saying. A man of science seeks the law, finds it, obeys it, and unimaginable power is in his hands. The same is true with a life of the spirit, if we learn and obey.

Prayer is not merely asking for things or even qualities; it is using the mental and emotional law by which we receive power to transform defeat into victory. "We do get energy, quiet, gentle, sure," said a man who was at the end of his row—his friends thought he was down and out from drink, but he won through faith.

Jesus had the power to awaken the faith capacity in people. All great souls have it in some degree. A talk with Phillips Brooks was like a spiritual blood transfusion to a man perplexed and tangled up. Often people forgot the trouble they came to see him about—they went out walking on air.

Vincent Sheean lost his faith, or thought he had. Two talks with Gandhi, just before he was shot, seemed to remake his very soul. Life became a new thing, radiant and vibrant. Contact with a man of faith, by a divine contagion, will often awaken in us "the power of an endless life."

How many folk today are lonely, fearful, bored, unhappy, sick of body or soul, tired of life and afraid of death. They need power to live their whole life, not just a tiny part of it. They have a capacity for faith, and it will work if only they will use it—go act upon it, whatever the risk.

"By grace are ye saved through faith," the Bible tells us times without end—saved from fear, futility, any dull death in life. Faith opens doors, unties our souls, and makes life the singing thing it ought to be.

WHEN A MAN PRAYS

"Behold, he prayeth." Acts 9:11

UPON THIS earth there is nothing more amazing than a man at prayer. An altar tells us something about man we can never forget.

"Life is short, nature is hostile, man is ridiculous," said Somerset Maugham, in the modern manner. No one denies the first item. Life is a flicker, the briefest thing, blown out before we are able to turn around. There is no time in its fleeting instant for anything but love.

At times nature is harsh and ruthless, like a roaring tempest, sweeping man away with flood and storm. At other times she is as gentle as a lamb—in the springtime with its delicious trouble in the ground; in the autumn with the mellow radiance on a friendly hill; in bird song and dawn and dusk.

Man is often ridiculous beyond words, in his belligerence, his greed, his incredible vanity; but he is also magnificent in his valor, his creativeness, his capacity to live—and die—for ideals, for the good of others, for a future his eyes will never see on earth.

Yes, man can be ridiculous—but not when he prays. His sensitivity to heavenly hauntings, his loneliness for a more human fellowship, his need for support from a source unseen, betrays a mystery even in his meanness, a glint of glory.

"Lord, thou hast made us for thyself, and our heart is restless till it rests in thee," a great saint wrote ages ago. Thus in one shining line we are told the story of the worshiper—that is, as the word means, man seeking the worth of life, the meaning of his brief and broken days.

Why does man pray? For the same reason that flowers grow and birds sing. As sparks ascending seek the sun, so the wistful, dreaming soul of man seeks its source; seeks to know whence it came and why, and what it is here to do. Man is truly wise only when he prays, broken as his prayer may be.

Of course he can be selfish, even cheap, in his prayer. Like Jacob and many another, he may try to bargain with God, agreeing to serve God if God will serve him and favor his fortune. But when he prays for others—even his enemy—his words take wings and soar to the heights.

> Prayer is the soul's sincere desire,
>   Uttered or unexpressed;
> The motion of a hidden fire
>   That trembles in the breast.

Think of the wonder of it! Like music, prayer deals directly with a reality too deep for words, with a realm greater than our little lives, as the sea is greater than the dewdrop. It speaks to God, the All-Wise, of needs and longings which reach out beyond life, time, and death.

Prayer unearths new riches. It releases new powers. It

A BELIEVING HEART

"Be not faithless, but believing." John 20:27

A BELIEVING heart is the most precious treasure of life. It saves us from the despair to which we are tempted, the dark thoughts we know not nor can name. It gives us courage to face the hard facts of life.

By the same token, to lose a believing heart is a bitter bereavement. It shuts so many doors. It erases our horizons. It ends in dull indifference, or that awful hardness which in our folly we mistake for wisdom.

Faith is not strain; it is respose. It is not make-believe. It is not credulity. It is not wishful thinking. It is not accepting ideas in spite of evidence. It is doing what we know to be right in face of all obstacles.

"Why don't you believe in God?" Tolstoi asked Gorki, abruptly, almost as if he had struck him a blow in the face. "I have no faith," replied Gorki, trying to make the answer as final and crushing as the question.

"It is not true," said Tolstoi. "By nature you are a believer and you cannot get along without God. You will realize it one day. You disbelieve because you have been hurt. The world is not what you like.

"There are also some people," he added, "who do not believe out of shyness. Faith, like love, requires courage and daring. One must say 'I believe'—and everything will explain itself to you. Faith is only a greater love; you must love still more, and then your love will turn to faith."

Tolstoi was right. Man was made for faith, a deep demanding faith. To believe is natural to him; skepticism is agony. When we lose faith, we deny our own nature; all is uncertainty—the bottom drops out of life.

If man denies the high, heroic faith of his race, he becomes the victim of every kind of false faith, as we see in our own day. When he turns away from God, he adopts a made mysticism of "race and soil and blood."

With uncanny insight the dictators saw that man needed and desired a new loyalty to fill his lonely, aimless life, so they gave him an insane faith. If man rejects the religion of heaven, he accepts the religion of hell.

Man is a child of God; if he loses that faith, he acts like a demon. Hence the human earthquakes of our times, a civilization set on fire, leaving trails of skeletons across the earth. Such is the incredible power of an evil, fanatical faith. It melts man into a mass, and makes him a weapon in the hands of an unscrupulous dictator. If evil faith is so mighty, a good faith is more powerful.

Faith is genius. No force on earth is equal to it. As Jesus said, a tiny grain of faith can remove mountains of difficulty. The word "impossible" is not in its vocabulary. It meets disaster but is not defeated.

Nearly every human being loses faith, but if he is wise, he finds it again. When the little boat of childish faith strikes the open sea, it is often wrecked by the storm of life. A traditional faith is not enough.

If we have courage to go on, trusting where we cannot

see, if we have the daring to fight and the patient humility to wait, we shall find a firmer, nobler faith.

Faith is tried to the very end. A dear old woman wrote to me, "My youth is gone, my hope is dead, my heart is heavy; but I neglect no duty—my trust in God holds."

One could reply only that though God had taken everything else—she had lost her two grandsons in war—in leaving her a love of righteousness, he had left her the best gift he had. If so much is true, more must be true.

"Lord, I believe; help thou mine unbelief," is one of the most moving prayers ever uttered. The man was asking Jesus to help his afflicted boy—he wanted to believe, he was trying to believe; he laid bare his heart, and ours.

No one can hear that cry, so poignant and pleading, and not feel akin to that far-off man in his woe, in his wish to believe, and in his bitter trial of faith.

Jesus accepted his believing unbelief, and healed his boy—so great is the power of faith, even when mixed with fear, dismay, and many doubts. To keep a believing heart, in spite of griefs and defeats, is the final wisdom.

It is not easy to do, heaven knows; but the alternative is ghastly. "Though he slay me, yet will I trust in him," said Job in the depth of his agony. The reward of his tenacious faith was rich beyond the power of words to tell.

The higher the faith, the harder it is to hold, but the more it is worth holding. At last, before we know it, the faith we hold, holds us—and will not let go, whatever storms of life may beat upon us.

TAKING CHANCES

"Time and chance happeneth to them all." Eccl. 9:11

Is THERE such a thing as chance or luck, good or bad? Is life in any sense a lottery? Do we win if we get the breaks, lose if we do not?

The answer is "Yes and no." On the lower levels of life the element of chance does enter our lives. Things do happen to us because we happen to be in a certain place at a certain time. But higher up it is not so.

Of course if we knew everything, all the factors involved in any event, chance might be ruled out. If when we flip a coin, we knew the weight of the coin, the resistance of the air, the position of the coin, the exact energy in tossing it, we could predict how it would fall.

Just so in life—if we knew all the facts and forces, we could tell how a thing would work out. Even one fact left out may upset the applecart. But we do not know everything about anything. Many a case in law or in medicine has been lost because one fact was overlooked. Only God is never surprised.

But the fact that God knows a thing will happen does not make it happen. It may be something he does not intend, but he allows it to happen in order to fulfill a larger purpose. Much that comes to pass is not the will of God, but he permits it because man must be free to err if he is to be man.

God wills good, only good, always, to everybody. But within the framework of his good will things happen which he did not intend and does not want. Like a stitch awry in the making of a rug, the supreme Artist takes the mistake or sin or sorrow and weaves it into his benign pattern.

Often we have a stroke of good luck, so we think, but as we know more about it, the less "luck" had to do with it.

A man had to visit the town where I lived. His train coming in was delayed, and he missed the train going out. He attended a service in my church. He did not make himself known.

Sometime later a pulpit was vacant in his city, and I was called to it—and accepted, wondering how it came to be. Two years later I visited a man in his last illness, and he told me how I came to be invited to the church. He attended my service, liked it, and thought of me for his church.

A part of the luck was explained, but only a part. He was a retired preacher, and knew a sermon when he heard one—so he said. But neither of us knew what delayed his train coming into town—a long series of happenings lay back of it, too intricate for any mortal to trace to the end.

Often what looks like good luck turns out to be not so good. Then too a bit of bad luck turns out for good, like the man who wrote the article "Thank God for My Heart Attack." It stopped him, made him reorder his life, and he found such happiness as he had never known before. If

Ignatius Loyola had not suffered a broken leg in battle, he might not have become a saint.

Some events, both good and bad, take place, for which neither God nor man is responsible, so we have to call them luck. But it is only a label for our ignorance. It is idle to make them an alibi for vanity, doubt, or despair. By fighting "bad luck" some of the greatest victories have been won. How often a handicap brings out something in people they had never imagined possible.

Faith is taking chances. My friend Donald Hankey said, "Religion is betting your life there is a God." Pascal had said it long ago. It is a sage bet, surely. One who takes the risk, and follows it through, amid good and ill, can win faith—knowledge beyond both proof and dispute. The highest truth "proves itself on our pulses," as Keats put it. We do not dream or guess; we know.

When Paul said, "I know whom I have believed," he did not mean that he had come to his certitude by argument. Not by logic, but by love; for since God is love, he is known only by love. A faith that goes no deeper than logic will not last, will not hold amid the bitter struggles of life.

In all the higher ranges of life there is an element of adventure. "Gambling, higher style," a famous preacher called it. Jesus was brave enough to believe the highest; he staked everything—even his life—upon it, up to the Cross and beyond. He seemed to lose, but we know that he won—for himself and us.

Often, alas, in the moral life men bet on the wrong horse. They think, gamblers as we are, all of us, that they can do evil and get away with it. But ever the law stands firm, unbreakable, "Whatsoever a man soweth, that shall he also reap"—that, not something else; more of the same kind. The harvest of our sowing makes our life a heaven or a hell—automatically, we may say.

Life on this earth cannot be lived on a basis of facts alone. Facts may point the direction, but we must take chances, go beyond facts—take "a mortal leap" by faith beyond fact, as Lord Kelvin tells us he did when he discovered new truth in science. He proved again that "faith is . . . the evidence of things not seen."

At the end time of life, when the lights go out and we face the dark, we take the grandest chance of all. We do not know, we cannot see, but it is best to believe the best. Wisdom is to trust the love of God.

SELF-INSPECTION IS HEALTHY

"What lack I yet?" Matt. 19:20

A RICH young man came to Jesus and asked what he should do to win eternal life. Jesus reminded him of the commandments, naming them. "All these things," he said, "have I kept from my youth up: what lack I yet?"

Jesus, "beholding him loved him," seeing that he was a fine, clean youth. Also, he was not satisfied, he wanted to go further. Jesus put him to a test; but he failed; he would not give up his possessions, and "he went away sorrowful."

A boy entered a drugstore and went into a telephone booth. The door was ajar, and the clerk overheard one side of the conversation.

"Is this the firm that advertised for a boy a few days ago?"

"Oh, the job has already been filled, has it?"

"Does the boy do his work to suit you? Thank you. Good-by."

"Tough luck that you missed out on that job," said the clerk, as the boy came out of the booth.

"Don't fool yourself," said the boy. "I landed the job three days ago. I'm just checking up."

A young man, fresh from college, went to the office of a businessman in New York, a friend of the family, to talk about his lifework. Suddenly the man turned to him and said, "Really, I question whether I have found any of this happiness they talk so much about. If it exists at all, I have never been able to hook it." He too was checking up.

A famous preacher tells how he tried to read one of his old sermons, but could not stick it out. He tried another, and it also fell flat. Something was wrong. At last he discovered to his surprise that his whole outlook had altered, like the shifting of a river bed, and his old sermons had nothing to say to him.

In a remarkable letter a woman told me how she saved her marriage from wreck when it was on the rocks. She blamed her husband, of course, but one day she sat down and asked herself some plain, blunt questions.

"If his secretary left him, he would be panic-stricken; if he lost one or two of his men friends, he would be heartbroken. But if I went away, what would he miss? I've been a selfish parasite." An honest checkup saved the day. It is a healthy thing, now and then, to face up to ourselves searchingly.

Years ago, while living in England, a dear old man told me how he dealt with himself, and I have never forgotten it. He was so gentle and wise, he must have felt my thought about him. Here is his story:

"Up until a few years ago," he said, in a rare mood of intimacy, "I was a most irritable man. When anything went wrong, I fussed and fumed and flew off the handle. My influence, such as it was, religious or otherwise, was worse than undone. I suffered in health, in business; I was miserable and made others miserable.

"One day I pulled myself up and said, 'Look here, you are just a plain fool.' In the Bible, as you know, it is a sin to call our brother a fool, but we are not forbidden to call ourselves a fool. 'You are a fool,' I said to myself, and I deserved it. 'If your religion, or failing that, if your common sense does not cure your fussy temper, what has it done for you? What is it worth?'

"In short, I gave myself a dose of fool-medicine, and it worked. I made up my mind that I would bring all my strength of will, and all the grace of God I could get, to bear upon my temper. While I do not want to boast, it has been a long time since I found myself fretting and worrying. I cannot tell you the difference it makes in my own life and in the happiness of others."

It made me think of a little poem by Robert Sill, in which he said he had often prayed, "God be merciful to me, a sinner," but more often his prayer had to be, "God be merciful to me, a fool." Is not foolishness a sin too?

Just a little self-attention, taking ourselves by the scruff of the neck, pulling ourselves up sharply, and telling ourselves the truth like a Dutch uncle, might save us from a lot of folly, not to mention cruelty.

If it were a physical ill, we would go to a doctor, get a checkup, and have it put right. What we need is a stiff dose of fool-medicine—nasty stuff, no doubt—to cure us of petty, silly sickness of soul.

All of us know quite well that our religious life is a meager affair, thin and stunted. Yet we do little about it, and let things drift. Without prayer, said Carlyle, there can be no religion, or only a dumb one. Our religion is often dumb, not only toward God, but toward our fellows also.

Let's have an inner checkup, seek a better-ordered religious life, and not try to live at random. Dull neglect means defeat in time of crisis; we need to do justly, to love mercy, and to walk humbly, softly, privately with God.

THE WORLD'S HEART

"He hath set the world in their heart." Eccl. 3:11

IN THE American Standard Version there is another reading of this text, more correct, "He hath set eternity in their heart." What amazing words!

Here is the origin and explanation of the meaning and mystery of life. If man has heaven-storming aspirations, if he thinks thoughts that wander through eternity, it is because there is a spark of God-fire in his heart.

Else he would be untroubled by faith, untormented, uninspired by the great dream of truth, beauty, and goodness. Life is from above downward, from within outward; it is its own best priest and prophet, if we listen in.

Religion is the heart of the world. Without it man ceases to be man. If he has nothing to bow down to, nothing serene and supreme, he bows down to himself, in pitiful self-idolatry—frustrated by his own vanity. If he loses his vision of God, even a palace becomes a dreary desert place, an aching emptiness.

Looking out over the world of his day, the prophet Jeremiah said, "There is sorrow on the sea; it cannot be quiet." It is the tragedy of our own day, if we listen where all its voices meet, "if we hear them sound together, if we hear them sob alone." A great ache comes up from the heart of the world.

Alas, religion, which ought to unite humanity and

heal it, is itself divided, not about great things but about little things. It majors in minors; it deals in "mint and anise and cummin," forgetting the weightier matters of law and love. If we make little things big, big things will appear little.

Now consider. In the Bible, as in our common speech, the "heart" is the seat of the emotions. As for man, "As he thinketh in his heart, so is he." Again, "Keep thy heart with all diligence; for out of it are the issues of life." Again, "With the heart man believeth unto righteousness"—so the wise old Bible tells us.

Right belief is of high value; but belief may be only opinion, and "opinion is not religion, not even right opinion," as Wesley taught us, since right opinion may be held in the wrong spirit, and become irreligious. Not until truth enters our hearts, sets fire to our feelings, does it influence us deeply.

Here is the difference between belief and faith: belief is truth held in the mind; faith is a fire in the heart. Until the highest we know or can think reaches and rules our emotions, we are not safe from doubt and disaster. Men "whose hearts God had touched," is how the Bible describes the prophets.

Emotion, deep feeling, is the power of life. It is like the steam in an engine, the gasoline in an automobile, which drives our lives for good or ill. Emotional control, direction, devotion is almost the secret of successful and noble living. That is why faith and prayer are so vital to inner stability and poise.

Our business is to desire what God desires for us, not to be ruled by our own vagrant whims. This demands discipline. To keep our hearts, despite the knocks and shocks of life, we must diligently avoid negative emotions, as we would avoid infections, for they can drive us to destruction.

Fear, envy, hate, jealousy, self-pity are so many forms of acid—they eat the heart out of us. How can a world so full of hate and fear and terror ever know God, much less serve him—hate hides his face, fear darkens the sky. Alas, much of the religion of the world is negative and deadening.

The great religions of the East, noble as they are and rich in beauty, are nearly all negative. They teach us to kill desire, to seek nothingness, not to fulfill our highest hopes. It is appalling, if we think about it. They end often in a benumbing quietism, or else in a dreary, dull fatalism.

By contrast, Jesus was always positive, affirming the worth and glory and promise of life. There is not a single note of despair in his words. "This do, and thou shalt live." He was both a mystic and an activist. "Thou shalt love thy neighbour." "Go, and do thou likewise." Such was ever his attitude and challenge.

Emotions unexpressed—not acted upon—turn inward, tie themselves in knots, twist themselves into tangles. We must express them, "get them off our chest," as we say, and that is what prayer is for. We can pour out our hearts to God, telling him things we can tell no human being, no matter how near.

Here is no pious exhortation; it is a law, a method of training our souls to receive and achieve serenity, power over dark moods—over fear, worry, and the things we call "nerves." The words of the prophet Isaiah are true: "Thou wilt keep him in perfect peace, whose mind is stayed on thee: because he trusteth in thee."

Restless we are, restless we shall be until we find our rest in God, who is nearer than our own souls. If we cannot trust God, there is nothing for us. If God be for us, with us, even within us, who can be against us, what can hurt us? Here is the great religion—to trust the love of God.

Will the troubled heart of the world ever know and trust this truth? Yes, it is not impossible; it is inevitable, when at last man grows up and learns the truth.

THE LISTENER

"He that hath ears to hear, let him hear." Mark 4:9

THESE WORDS run like a refrain through all the teaching of Jesus, and like all his words, they might have been spoken this morning.

Too often, if we go to church, we feel that it is up to the preacher to make us listen. If he cannot hold our interest, if he cannot "get it across," it is just too bad for him. We do not feel that we have lost anything anyway.

Indeed, we think of the preacher as a salesman trying to sell us something we neither need nor want very much, but which we might consider if we are approached nicely enough, but otherwise our minds wander.

But with Jesus it was not so. He placed the emphasis on hearing, reminding people of their responsibility in listening. "If any man have ears to hear, let him hear," he said. "Take heed what ye hear." And again, "Whosoever heareth these sayings of mine, and doeth them, I will liken him unto a wise man, who built his house upon a rock, . . . and it fell not."

With him the preacher is not a performer, but a herald. The question is not whether he has a nice voice, a good presence, an enchanting personality, but whether he has the Word of God. A sermon is not a thing on which an entertainment tax ought to be paid; it is the truth about life and how to live it.

Alas, in our day the earth has become an auditorium, a whispering gallery, a chamber of echoes. Voices are everywhere; the din is deafening. It is a noisy, newsy, gossipy world, a babel of confused cries and alarms. What men say is not wiser than of yore, but everybody hears everything.

To learn how to be silent and listen in a noisy world is almost the secret of life. All knowledge, all art, all invention, all religion is the result of listening in on the universe. There is something almost pathetic in the attitude of nature holding out her mysteries, teasing our curiosity.

One day Edison heard a slight unusual sound in a project on which he was working. He stopped and studied it, and thus invented the phonograph. As Huxley said, the attitude of the man of science should be to sit down before the facts, intent, alert, forgetting himself, and listen in simplicity and humility.

Such is also the attitude of religion, as of old the people asked Moses to go near and listen for them in the place of hearing. "Speak thou unto us all that the Lord our God shall speak unto thee; and we will hear it, and do it." Such is the mission of the poet, the seer, the prophet who listens to the "still small voice," as Elijah did at Mount Horeb, when the storm had passed and gone.

"Who heareth me shall not be confused," to which the psalmist made answer, "I will hear what the Lord will say in me." These words were the text of the famous sermon on

"True Hearing," by Eckhart, in which he learned the truth. "There is something in the soul that is a blood relative of God."

How can we ever pay our debt to the great quietists, the listeners, waiting in an "intense stillness" to hear the truth? As one of them said, "Who listens to the divine voice is delivered from many unnecessary conceptions"—things about which we argue endlessly. And Newman added these wise words:

> It is thy very energy of thought,
> Which keeps thee from thy God.

Here is the secret of much of our spiritual confusion and poverty—we talk so much and listen so little. Prayer is more than petition; it is also listening for the answer. Too often we tell God what we want, when we want it, how we want it, as if we knew more than he knows, dictating to him.

All real leaders of men are still, strong men who know how to listen and wait. They hear not only what people are saying, but what they are really thinking—often a very different thing. They hear what the soapbox orator says; they also study the image of the future in the minds of the poets.

Workers we need, but listeners too, if ever we are to get men out of the slums, and the slums out of men—a much harder thing to do. Indeed, in the field of human relations, now so tangled and awry, in the home, in industry, in the nation, our greatest need is to listen in on other lives and learn.

How many marriages could be saved from wreck by listening in, each trying honestly to understand the other as well as himself. If we tried it more often, irritation would give way to a hush in our hearts—the rain water would run away, and the deep springs of affection would flow.

"Be still, and know that I am God," or better, "Let me be God, not you." If religious leaders would obey that wisdom, they would hear, underneath their rites and forms which divide, a dateless river of faith flowing through the ages, the one great religion, the life of God in the soul of man.

In the town of Shechem in the Holy Land, where Jesus talked with the woman by the well, in the daytime one hears the hum of bazaars and the voices of children at play. But at night in the silence one hears the sound of underground rivers flowing in the stillness—it is a parable.

Evermore, for each of us—we who fail so much and make a poor fist in our fight for the highest—the words of Jesus still speak with a wisdom that is truly wise, "If any man have ears to hear, let him hear."

WHAT WE WANT

"He gave them their request; but sent leanness into their soul." Ps. 106:15

WHAT IS all the world seeking? What do men and nations want more than anything else? What is the desire of all races and peoples?

Of course the world wants many things—wealth, health, power, pleasure, prestige, and trinkets no end. It wants "life, liberty, and the pursuit of happiness."

But the one word which sums up the desires of all peoples is "security." Men think that if they had security, all other things would be added. They could win health, wealth, happiness, power, and progress.

But is it true? No. Too much security is as bad as too little, if not worse. If all our dreams came true, if we had everything we wanted, would we be satisfied and happy? Far from it. Unless we want the right things.

Else boredom would become a blight, as it is today. How dreary to have no more dreams, no desires to drive us to effort, no aims or ideals to lure us. The end would be dry rot, decay, and the most dismal banality.

A picturesque short story puts the truth vividly. A man killed in an auto accident awoke in a strange, silent place. "Is anybody here?" he cried.

Instantly an angel stood before him, "What can I do for you, sir?" The man asked what he could have. "Anything you like," the angel explained.

"That is, anything except one," the angel added. "There is no pain here, no struggle, no want."

The man was delighted. "Fine," he said. "Take forty years off my life; I have come to the right place." And it was done. Then followed a list of things he wanted, and everything he asked was granted.

After a time he got tired of getting everything he wanted, when he wanted it. He was so bored he could not go on. "I want something to do," he said, "some effort, even pain. I'd rather be in hell than be here."

The angel was startled, and replied, "Where do you think you are? This is hell!"

By what delusion of mind can we embrace the fallacy that more and better things alone can make better people and living? By what twist of logic can we ignore the truth that "man does not live by bread alone"? It is absurd—quantities of things instead of qualities of spirit.

The Slender Reed, exquisitely written, posing many basic questions, tells the story of a woman in her early forties who had all the symbols of security: a good husband, a charming daughter, and every kind of comfort. Yet she felt ill at ease, inadequate. She seemed to believe that her security depended on other people and her surroundings.

Then slowly one by one the artificial props of her unhappy life were removed. Her husband died, her daughter married, and she gradually lost her fortune. With a strength which amazed her she gave up the last shred of her security, leaving her home of many years.

Then she pondered her situation. There had never been any real safety there. Shelter, yes, and protection of a sort—from the weather at least. But there is no protection in any house from the things which are already in it. The thing called security, so talked about, did it really exist?

No, she concluded, there is no such thing in the world. Not against old age, or against illness, or loneliness, or heartache. Then for the first time she felt safer than she had for many, many years. Because she knew that there is no safety anywhere, it was foolish to count on it.

Few people, if any, can have life on their own terms. We must take life on its own terms, and not expect from it what it cannot give—much less hunger for better bread than can be made out of wheat. It is idle to build a dream house for ourselves; it is certain to be shattered.

Only in the life of the spirit, daringly lived, is there any security of soul, any serenity of soul. Faith alone can defeat and conquer fear. Trust in God, and the courage to meet whatever life gives us—this is the secret of inner security, and if we have inner peace, wild and whirling events cannot dismay us.

Many of the loftiest leaders of faith lived in stormy, dangerous times. Jesus knew no outward security; he did not ask it. Neither did Francis of Assisi or Gandhi. "In quietness and in confidence shall be your strength," Isaiah told us, he who lived when the world was shaking and falling to pieces.

THREE BIG QUESTIONS IN LIFE

"In that day ye shall ask me nothing." John 16:23

THORNTON WILDER had a lovely play some years ago, also made into a motion picture, entitled *Our Town.* The play is packed with spiritual understanding, like everything that he has written.

In the play, Emily, in her illness, passed out of her body far enough and long enough to see life from another angle and a better perspective. She brought back with her three questions, which go to the bottom of human living.

First question: Do any human beings ever realize life while they live it? A few do, a very few—some people do see the sheer wonder of living, grasp it and live it; they do not put off living as so many of us do.

Most of us are afraid to live, afraid to take the risks; too tame, too timid, too lazy to make the venture; afraid of ourselves and others. We do not see life until it has passed; as was said of a greatly beloved President.

President Coolidge worked hard, saved, planned, reached the highest office, then retired and wanted to play and rest. But it was too late. Not long after he retired he died suddenly.

Youth does not see the beauty of youth—its boyish grace, its maiden magic—as age sees it. A boy does not see himself as his father sees him, still less as his grandfather sees him with the clearer, kinder eyes of age.

No doubt that is why, when we get older, we long for

"the good old days." We forget the tensions of the past; we want to go back, settle down, and live it. One reason is that perhaps there is no fear in the past; it has gone.

Hazlitt, the essayist, after failing at painting, marrying a minx, quarreling with his friends, being overworked, gnawed by debt, and suffering from indigestion, died saying, "I have had a happy life." He had forgotten.

The second question is equally penetrating: Are we always at the mercy of one self-centered passion, or another? Most of us are, most of the time—even romantic love is often a self-centered passion when it seems to center in another.

Love of money, political ambition, lust for power, or the many varieties of vanity blind us to the beauty of life. Some one thing gets so close to us that we cannot see anything else—not even life itself.

The third question is profound and searching: Don't we ever come really close to another? Is it impossible to get out of ourselves into the lives of others? Are we shut up, as prisoners in the solitary confinement of our cells?

The fight against loneliness begins early, and goes on to the end. We can get just so close to other people—even those we love best—then we are stopped; a door closes, we hear it click, and we cannot open it.

But we can get closer to God than to anyone else, if we know how and take time to do it. And so religion—or whatever word we use to describe this inner necessity—is not simply important, but deeply vital.

But enough. A great poet has told us that life is just an opportunity to learn how to pray, and prayer cancels loneliness. When we learn how to pray, we find One "closer . . . than breathing, and nearer than hands and feet."

No wonder so many people try to run away from this inner loneliness; they are afraid of it—they do not know how to be alone, without being so lonely that it makes the heart ache.

They want to be going places, doing things, mistaking excitement for pleasure; anything to escape being alone. A story I read as a boy told of a strange request a father made in his will to his son; I never forgot it.

It asked him to put on his best suit and sit alone in the best room of his home half an hour each day. He obeyed the request. At first he felt foolish, just sitting alone; then he came to love it and to look forward to it.

Slowly he learned the wisdom of the request. He began to think, to put things together in his mind into a pattern; he learned to be alone without being lonely. In other words, he mastered one of the fine arts of life.

We have to live with ourselves whether we like it or not, and until we can live with ourselves without friction, we cannot live with others and keep the peace. Here is half the trouble with marriages that go on the rocks.

How to live, how to handle our minds, is the one matter; and these three questions from Thornton Wilder's play, if we ponder and try to answer them, will help us in the great business of learning how to live.

IN THE SUMMER

"Thou hast made summer and winter." Ps. 74:17

SURELY IT ought to be easy for all men to have faith in God in the summertime. In these glad, these great, these goodly days the beauty of the Lord our God is upon us, and "earth's crammed with heaven."

The attributes of summer are light, beauty, and overflowing life; and these are also the attributes of God. No wonder we are moved by a feeling, so deep that it defies analysis, that here is the unveiling of God.

So it has been as far back as human records run. Since time began, the ritual of the seasons, moving with unbroken rhythm, has stirred the heart of man in every age to thoughts of confidence and wonder and worship.

In summer the grass covers the earth like a soft robe, the flowers keep their faithful tryst, the birds chant a chorus of praise at dawn and an evening hymn at twilight. Truly we are dead of heart if we do not join in.

But if there is summer glow and glory, there is also winter with its ice and snow, its sleet and slush, and its cutting winds. What of its bleak days when the trees are skeletons, the earth is bare, and the flowers are dead?

Ages ago men held that there were two rival deities, always at war. Only so could they explain the contrasts amid which they lived. Not so the wise old Bible, with its vision of the unity of the world, its faith in the God who made summer and winter, light and darkness, life and death.

For in winter nature is not dead, but sleeps, and in her dreams she designs all the shapes which life and beauty take in the summer. In December she fashions June, as out of a Cross a crown of rejoicing is made.

For winter is not dead, not inert, it is atingle with life and aglow with prophecy. It is the loom on which summer splendor is woven. Summer explains winter, fulfills it, justifies its hardship. Just so it is in the life of man, in which light and shadow, joy and pain, are interwoven.

Thus the seasons of the soul match the seasons of the year, if we have eyes to see and a heart to understand. Winter stores up power, its snow purifies, its harshness puts a finer tone of fortitude into the heart.

How radical at times are the fluctuations of fortune. The patriarch Job had a long summer of health, wealth, and happiness. Then came the winter blast, sweeping everything away, leaving him penniless and in pain. But Job learned that the same God who had given had taken away; "Blessed be his name."

History, too, has its winter winds and its summer zephyrs. What a black winter we have lived through. But "if winter comes, can spring be far behind," if we have the faith and courage to wait? Slowly but surely the faint signs of spring come in the air, frail hopes of green fields promising the golden, waving grain.

In his diary Thoreau, prophet of the out-of-doors, wise in the lore of living things, wrote words of blended meditation and prayer worthy of being framed and hung up in our hearts, as so many of his words are:

> I wish to begin this summer well; to do something worthy and wise; to transcend my daily routine; to have my immortality now. I pray that this summer may be fair in my memory. May I dare as I have never done. May I purify myself anew as with fire and water, soul and body. May nothing beautiful escape me. A man should be something worthier at the end of the year than at the beginning.

Keats and Plato agreed that there is more beauty in the world than is needed for its own end. They felt that God has embosomed us in beauty the better to entangle us in divine meditations, and thus to draw us to himself. What sermons in stone, what books in running brooks, if we have hearts to hear.

For summer is not an end in itself; it is a prophecy. It is fleeting, and looks toward the autumn harvest. For this the birds sing, the flowers bloom, and the sunlight falls aslant the trees and ripples on flowing waters.

Soon the summer will be ended. What then? What will the harvest of our lives be? What handful of grain will our days, fleeting and few, bring to the Lord of the harvest? Aye, there is a matter to be pondered in our hearts.

WORRIED HUMANITY

"Thou art . . . troubled about many things. Luke 10:41

A RECENT essay was entitled *This Worried Mankind.* It exactly describes the state of mind in our fear-haunted, worrying world.

In such a world, if we are to save our sanity, we must learn to take care of our minds. Else we may fall into the habit of a feverish, fretful, gnawing anxiety, which will poison our lives and unfit us for our tasks. A virus will seep into our very souls and paralyze us before we know it.

Some things we ought to worry about, or at least feel a concern. They are dangerous; but we must think of them with our minds, not with our emotions, much less with our imaginations. The trouble is that we worry about too many things, most of which really do not matter, and that is a waste.

To worry about the world as we do, carrying it on our backs, is futile. It is too big, too heavy, and in any case it is not our job. Now and then it is torn to pieces and put together in another pattern. But there is little that we can do about it, except refuse to be scared out of our wits.

For one thing, we can wait until a thing happens before we worry about it. There will be plenty to worry about then, but we shall worry about facts, not about phony fears. Besides, it may not happen, but if it does, other things will happen, modifying the setting and altering the consequences.

Walking in a lovely English estate years ago, from garden to garden, I saw one sign everywhere, "Please Shut This Gate." Those four words are a whole philosophy and a wise strategy. Shut the gate on old griefs and grievances, old blessings and blunders—they are gone, let them go.

Lloyd George said that the secret of his success was that he learned early in life to close every gate through which he passed. "Let the dead bury their dead," said Jesus. Shut out yesterday; one cannot go back, why live back—reliving things, doubling our load, shedding idle tears?

Also, we must learn to throw off things, as Paul threw off the venomous insect which fastened itself on his hand. He threw it in the fire before it could sting him. Some thoughts, some emotions are poisonous; they stick like burs and sting like bees. Throw them out of mind quickly.

In the same way, we must decide things, not let them dangle and dally. To drift is to be in hell, to steer is to be in heaven, said a wise man. The hours, the days we spend, not knowing what to do! Around and around we go, in slow, stagnant uncertainty.

It makes us weary and wears us down unless we learn to make up our minds, cut the knot, and get things done. Else we live hung-up, frightened, and confused. If we make a decision, then by way of reward or retribution, our decision will make or break us. Mistakes are costly, but the worst mistake is to make no decision, to just drift and dawdle.

"Forgetting those things which are behind," was a part of the wisdom of Paul. It is indeed a high art, else the past may clog the present and defeat the future. Some things Paul found it hard to forget—they hurt him—but he dropped them and pressed forward, "unto those things which are before."

A wise old saint prayed, "Lord, teach us to forget the things we ought not to remember, and to remember the things we ought not to forget." We need not wait until spring to clean house, but sort our old memories and throw away the litter, lest it clutter our minds.

It is not easy to manage our memories. Sad memories and happy memories hurt us equally, but in different ways. Yet is is possible to deal with them so they will not hurt us emotionally—they become like pictures on the wall. They no longer break our hearts.

"Somehow, I never thought it paid," said Lincoln when his friends urged him to reply to bitter, untrue words spoken against him. In such matters he was divinely absent-minded, and therein he was wise. Too wise to hate or worry, he learned to pray, as few men have ever learned.

Don't worry—pray! A simple religious faith, rightly and faithfully used, is the cure for more ills of body and mind than anything else on earth. Prayer, if we learn the art and practice of it, can work wonders, giving us a peace of heart which the world can neither give nor take away.

It steadies us, holds us together. It helps us to think clearly, giving us a calm over-all view of our problem. It enables us to see all around it. It makes us forget ourselves. It shifts our attention to more enduring things. It heals our hurts, gives strength, opens doors.

Too many lights of prayer have gone out, leaving us in the dark. In a world of whispering dreams and wistful dust, why mar the wonder of life with futile fears, cares, and regrets. Learn to pray!

THE THREE R'S

"Study to be quiet." Thess. 4:11

IN RELIGION, as in education, there are three R's. They are the rudiments of the best life, its alphabet, which we must master. Else we cannot even start to climb the ladder of faith toward our goal.

First, we must learn to *relax,* to let down, to unwind our nerves, to untangle our emotions. It takes time and practice, but we can learn to relax our body and sleep, lest the cares which infest the day infect the night, and we wake up tired of the day before it begins.

Otherwise something may snap. Life is tense today; we are hung up and strung up by every kind of tension. Our own affairs get twisted; all the scrambled, fear-driven world pours in on us. It is too much, even for the toughest of us.

In the morning we are busy about many things, active and aggressive, as we have to be. In the afternoon we go to a symphony concert, but we must lay aside our active mood and listen. We have been aggressive; now we must be passive. We have been doing something to our world; now we must let another world of melody do something to us—else even music cannot help us.

Just so it is in worship. If we carry our active mood into prayer, we are defeated by our eager, intense, urgent attitude, "God, give me what I want!" It may be something utterly unselfish we are praying for. But unless we pray receptively, responsively, listening, it cannot be given to us.

"Study to be quiet"; undress your mind as you do your body. Lay aside the cares of the day, adjourn the go-getter mood; learn to be still, and know that God is God, not you. "Thy will be done" is the supreme prayer; we are not to be back-seat drivers, dictating what God shall do.

If in prayer we try to force our selfish will upon the world, we fail. That is not religion; it is magic—trying to use God, not to let ourselves be used by him. Prayer is not a spare tire to be used when others things fail. It is not trying to move the arm of God, but letting his arm move us. For we are here on earth to do the will of God, not to live our own lives, or have our own way.

Second, in a relaxed and listening mood we must *realize* what life is, its worth and wonder. How little we think of this swift and awful gift of life, what it means and can mean. We are so busy making a living that we do not see what a marvel just living really is. Life is much greater than the little things that vex us, wasting our strength.

This is what it means to meditate—to turn truths over in the mind, like gems, studying their many facets. It is thus that we make truth true in us, true for us, translating faith into truth. In the nighttime the psalmist meditated on the law of God, and found peace and security.

"Now are we the sons of God, and it doth not yet appear what we shall be: but we know that, when he shall appear, we shall be like him; for we shall see him as he is." That is realizing the greatness of the soul, and to what fine issues it can ascend. Religion is the best cure for an inferiority complex. Sons of God, and if sons, "heirs; heirs of God, and joint heirs with Christ."

Life for most of us, most of the time, is made up of little things—little duties, little cares, little joys. But we must not think of life itself as a little thing. We must see its great background, and do little things in a great manner.

Third, it is not enough to relax and to realize; we must also *resolve,* in our hearts, to make our lives worthy of our heredity from God, not vaguely but specifically; we must set ourselves by God's grace to dig up and do away with the things that mar our lives and hold us back from the best.

Erasmus said of Dean Colet that he was a man of genuine piety, but he was not born with it. He was naturally hot, quick-tempered, impetuous, resentful, fond of pleasure, disposed to make a joke of everything. But he fought his faults, one by one, by study and fasting and prayer—and he won.

At last by the practice of salvation his whole soul was transfigured, and Erasmus could add, "I never knew a sunnier nature." Health of soul in this world of infections and illusions asks for such effort, alertness, and patience. Yet how little we seek a better-ordered inner life.

It is an old and simple technique, often tried—*relax, realize, resolve*—an art each of us can use for the health of his soul, anywhere, everywhere. But if we yield to inertia, and just drift along not making the extra effort to keep our hearts responsive, we drop to a lower level.

May God teach us how to live, how to love, how to pray, how to do good!

DEALING WITH FEAR

"Why are ye so fearful? How is it that ye have no faith?"
Mark 4:40

FEAR HATH torment," the Bible tells us. Even Solomon with all his wisdom was the victim of "fears in the night." He kept a band of armed men outside his door, with swords drawn, but fears got by and crept in.

Today we live in a frightened world. Horror of the past and terror of the future grip us. International conferences wrangle about rules, and the war of nerves goes on. H. G. Wells died in despair—he who had been so hopeful.

To a grim list of fears has now been added the threat of atomic energy, making a dark horizon. The four freedoms have not been won, least of all freedom from fear. It is idle to whittle down facts to fit fancy.

How shall we deal with fear, new and old? There are really four ways of handling fear, the first and most futile of which is funk. But funk is failure, it gives up the fight, and sinks into a kind of pitiful paralysis.

Wells said that the human mind is at the end of its tether. We need a new social mind to meet a new situation, but that new mind has not been developed. He saw no hope that man would make a jump to a higher level.

A leader of the science-save-us cult, he felt that science had betrayed us, piling fear upon fear. The mind of man has not kept pace with the new and strange powers unveiled by science; only destruction lies ahead.

Equally futile it is to resort to flight, to try to escape from the shadow of fear. A man in London said that he hated to see women standing in a trolley car. "What do you do about it?" he was asked. He replied, "I close my eyes."

Since the days of Jonah, the prophet, men have been trying to run away from fact, duty, and fear. But today there is nowhere to go, since the whole world is wrapped in a pall of fear. Mental flight is only fooling ourselves.

Life's being intolerable and insecure, ugly and brutal, we try to put it out of mind and have done with it. But in fact we only push it down into the mind. There it festers and poisons the soul. Unfaced fear may mean disaster.

No wonder mental ill-health runs rampant. When we try to fly from our fears, we find ourselves fighting specters of the mind. At last we touch off an explosion of some kind, and our lives are blown to pieces before we know it.

Since flight is useless—because we take our fears with us—there is another way open. We can fight our fears. Here plain pluck comes into play; it refuses to give in or give up. Courage is the first virtue.

Courage is not the absence of fear, but it refuses to let fear interfere with life. It can "take it" and come back for more; it can meet defeat and not be defeated. Many a frail little woman faces fear with unbelievable grit.

At least, if we have courage, we can face our fear long enough to find out what kind of fear it is. That is, whether it is fear of something really dangerous, or self-fear projecting itself on something not actually dangerous.

If we isolate our fear, bring it out into the open, we can see it for what it is. To know the facts is not weakness; it is wisdom. Also, since most of our fears are learned, they can be unlearned, if we take time to do it.

But even the finest courage gets tired and wears thin unless it is upheld and aided by the "something beyond courage," of which Lady Montagu wrote in a letter. Alas, her paper ran out and she did not tell us what she meant.

But we know what she meant. Neither funk, flight, nor fighting fear with bare hands can do the trick. As a friend of mine put it picturesquely, "Fear knocked at the door. Faith opened it, and lo! there was no one there!"

"Faith is the antiseptic of the soul," Walt Whitman wrote in his quiet way. Faith disinfects us from those dark dismays, akin to despair, which make us long for some honorable way out of life.

Faith and fear cannot live in the same heart. When faith fails, fear crawls in, a vile and clammy thing, cold, too, as we well know. When faith comes back, fear is ousted—kicked out the window, booted out the door.

But the faith that masters fear is more than belief, more than opinion, more than tradition. It is a living force, an act of adventure which commits us to a course of living and thinking, at once to a task and a trust.

As Josiah Royce said—he who knew such atrocious suffering toward the end—faith is finding that, in our own soul and in God, which meets and masters anything that life or death can do to us! Happily, he found it and won out.

The early Christians lived in a terrifying time when the world was falling to pieces. As someone has said, they looked at the world and saw reason for despair; they looked at God and "saw naught but an immeasurable hope."

It was in a day of doom that Augustine wrote his *City of God.* This lesson is for us, walking a knife-edge of crisis on the brink of chaos. "How is it that ye have no faith?" a sweet voice asks each of us. What is our answer?

ON THE RIGHT SIDE

"Cast the net on the right side of the ship." John 21:6

SOME PEOPLE are deaf on one side, and if we talk to the deaf ear, we waste our time. Some are blind on one side, and all appeals to that eye are in vain.

We have to discover the right approach or we fail. Hence the old saying, "Keep on the right side of every man." There is an approachable side, if we can find it—a side which will appreciate our efforts and respond, if we can reach it. Often it takes time, tact, and skill.

All of us have known people who are gruff, silent, grim, forbidding; we are afraid they will not only bark but bite. To have to study a man to learn how to approach him, and blame ourselves if we fail, is not pleasant.

To blunder along in our own way, and then lay all the fault for our failure on others, is natural and easy. Some go blundering ahead all their days, regardless of results, rubbing people the wrong way, making bad matters worse.

Hamilton Fyfe, in a story, tells what he learned as a salesman. He soon learned that it is never wise to go to the front door. Either they will not answer at all, or after a long wait one hears a bolt being undone. Then the door opens a few inches, and is slammed in his face.

Very wisely he found it better to go to the side door, or better still, the back door, where there is less suspicion and delay. Usually the back door was open and he could say what he had to say about his wares.

The front door, he said, is a pretense, a bluff, and we must not mistake the stern face for the real man, or hauteur for the true woman. They are human, kindly, friendly, if we take time to go to the side or back door.

In other words, we must adjust ourselves to other people, not attempt to adjust them to ourselves. Much of the trouble in human relations lies here—we want people to fit into our pattern, to stay in the pigeonhole where we put them.

Some seem to think that if we go at folk hammer and tongs, even if they are deaf on both sides, they will still catch our meaning. But that is an error; we may alienate them entirely, and never be able to reach them.

How angry it makes us when anyone goes at us in that fashion. Even if we were sympathetic with what they desire, their method closes all doors. We resent their tactics even when we are friendly to their idea. How much injury such people do good causes by their clumsy methods.

It is easy to find homes where the father and mother complain that their children will not listen to them—the parents are appealing to the deaf side of their children. They are on the wrong side of them.

Often teachers and preachers make the same mistake; people will not listen to them, or listening, they pay no heed. Mark Twain may have been wise when he built his home in Hartford—he put the back doors in front!

Too often we throw up our hands saying, "We have done everything we could." As if there were no "right side" in some cases. It may be hard to find, barricaded by long-seated suspicion or covered by prejudices, habits, and fears. Yet it is there, if only we can locate it.

The city of Mansoul may be a walled city, heavily guarded pride will not open its gates, flattery will not always unlock it, nor entreaty nor threat. It cannot be reached from above, but only on the level.

An American officer told me how he was a guest in an English home during World War II. He was received at the front door with a rather formal courtesy, as befitted an officer and a stranger. He felt rather ill at ease.

At dinner a delicious English tart was served, and that gave him his cue. He praised the tart as a kind of cousin of our American pie, which he described as "a tart with a cap on." Then he added, "The pie touch did it," and an evening which threatened to be formal, if not frosty, turned out to be congenial.

Jesus had rare skill in finding the "right side" of people; he seldom failed to open doors. He never treated any two people alike, as if one formula would always work. He knew that people are different, and he treated them so.

Said William James, "There may be very little difference between men, but that difference is very important." Indeed yes; it may mean the difference between success and failure in dealing with our fellow men.

Now that the ends of the earth are drawn together—jammed together—the problem of human relations is vitally important. If we fail here, we fail utterly. We must learn to find the "right side" of people.

LIFE'S TEMPTATIONS

"Lead us not into temptation." Matt. 6:13

THE GOSPEL in the Prayer Book for the first Sunday in Lent is the story of the temptation of Jesus. Only Jesus himself could have told the story of that deep inner crisis when he had to decide the purpose and method of his life.

No one else knew of that lonely struggle in the wilderness. Even Jesus was not exempt from temptation—a real temptation it was, too. He was tempted to take the short cut, and do quickly what can be done only slowly.

How should he use his power? To turn stones into bread and feed people—himself and others who are hungry? Jesus was very sensitive about hunger. He could not bear for people to be without food; again and again he fed the hungry.

Or should he employ a miracle, or even magic, to win his way? Or should he even appease evil, bow down to the devil, to gain conquest? Fortified by wise Bible words, Jesus resisted. He took the long, hard way, which is the only way.

In other words, Jesus was tempted by the good. Why should we think that it is only evil that tempts men? Strong men are tempted by their strength, weak men by their weakness. Jesus was tempted by the will of God—and yielded.

"Lead us not into temptation" is the most baffling phrase in the Lord's Prayer. It seems to imply that God tempts us;

but that is not true if by temptation we mean enticement to do evil. The words of the Bible are plain: "Let no man say when he is tempted, I am tempted of God: for God cannot be tempted with evil, neither tempteth he any man: but every man is tempted, when he is drawn away of his own lust, and enticed." When desire becomes lust, we are in danger.

"A series of right desires," is how a great saint described the Lord's Prayer. To desire the things we ought to desire is the secret of great living. But all of us are tempted, in the sense of being tested. The testing comes early and stays late—it never ends. Each of the "seven ages" of life has its own kind of testing—youth, middle age, old age, each is tested in its own way. No wonder we shrink from the testings of life.

Hence the phrase in the great idiom reads, "Let us not yield to temptation," or, "Grant that we fail not in the time of testing." It is a prayer not to escape testing, but for strength to overcome it.

Every man, every woman is tested, often terribly—testing is no respecter of persons, or professions, or creed, or station, or color, or race. Sometimes life tries us as if by fire, sometimes by cold and almost calculated frigidity.

Yet the wise old Bible tells us that no temptation, no testing, comes to us except "such as is common to man"; for God will not suffer us to be tempted above that we are able to bear, and "will with the temptation also make a way to escape."

These are great words, to be taken to heart, even if they rob us of the vanity of thinking that we are tempted more than anyone else. No, it is the common human lot—none of us would be worth his salt without such testing!

It is one thing to be tempted; it is another thing to yield. By the same token, we should have a rich and wise charity for those who fail in the tests of life; we too have "tried a little and failed much," as a great poet reminds us.

Maxwell Anderson in his drama *Valley Forge* has a scene in which Washington is tempted to betray his people. It was a test, but no enticement—not for a split second. Washington was tempted by the liberty of his people!

Whoever else might turn traitor and sink into self-seeking, that would Washington never do! Nothing could turn him aside from his dream of "a new nation, conceived in liberty, and dedicated to the proposition that all men are created equal," as Lincoln put it.

What are the greatest temptations in life? One is to turn cynic, to think cheaply of ourselves and others, to take the low view of human nature. Often facts seem to be in favor of that view, but it is false.

To yield to this way of thinking, always to expect the worst, not to trust our fellows, poisons life, makes us hard and bitter. When we lose faith in humanity, as we are often tempted to do, we lose our way in a dark country.

"The mass of men lead lives of quiet desperation," said Henry Thoreau. As we grow older, it is more so—we are tempted to despair, to give way to a dull, hopeless, dark gloom. Well may we pray, "Let us not yield to this temptation!"

It means a set, gray, apathetic end, an inertia more to be dreaded than the weight of years. The lights go out—we hate change, we suspect new ideas, our faith grows dim. From such an end may God in mercy deliver us!

But who is qualified to lecture another? Life tests all of us, whether we are gold or silver, or wood, or hay and stubble.

BECOMING SOMEBODY

"Power to become the sons of God." John 1:12

WHAT a thing can become is hinted to us in what it is. We do not expect an acorn to become a pear tree, or a pig to write a poem. "Boys will be boys," we say, meaning a kiddish prank which only boys would ever think of.

Boyd Edwards, famous headmaster, took this familiar saying about boys, and changing one word, made it the title of an arresting book, *Boys Will Be Men.* Of course we know that boys will become men, but a tremendous fact is suggested by the word "become." It is the wonder and mystery of growth!

Of Jesus it was said, "As many as received him, to them gave he power to become." Become what? "The sons of God," and as Paul adds, if sons, "then heirs; heirs of God, and joint-heirs with Christ." Did anyone ever hear of a legacy more fabulous; a destiny, a possibility more challenging and amazing?

It is like a check made out to us, signed by him, with the amount left blank for us to fill in. How we need to get rid of our timidity, our unbelief, our inferiority complex, stand erect, then fill in the check when our mind is clearest, our heart purest and least afraid, and our aspirations at their highest.

Think of the disciples of Jesus, just ordinary men—fishermen, taxgatherers, and the like—made extraordinary by their faith in him and their fellowship with him. If it had not been for Jesus, their names would never have been heard of. They became movers of the world, and writers of immortal books.

There was something like radium or atomic energy in the personality of Jesus, "stepped down," as the electricians say; something penetrating, healing, revolutionary. It made people over, made them taller of soul, rearranging their very being. To touch his spirit made all life new, glad, radiant, and it is still true.

All through his life Jesus laid emphasis upon growth, "becoming," not upon sudden spectacular experiences. The kingdom of heaven, he said, is like leaven or yeast in bread, slow, silent, sure. It is like planting a seed, first the blade, then the bloom, and at last the full-grown grain of wheat —so souls grow and unfold.

There is an old, old saying—no one knows who said it first, but Rufus Jones said it last—like this, "Our greatest object in life is to find the rest of ourselves." He also defined religion as "a process of becoming," of completion, finding and filling out what is lacking in our nature; really growing up.

How can we grow up spiritually? "As many as received him, to them gave he power." How can we receive power to become what we want to be? It is not handed to us in a package; we must "obey the law of the power, and the power will obey us." The early Christians called themselves "athletes of the spirit"—here is our cue.

Glenn Clark gave us his life story, *A Man's Reach,* taking its title from Browning's lines:

> a man's reach should exceed his grasp,
> Or what's a heaven for?

As a human record it is thrilling, the more because here is a man who talks religion, but does not talk about it—he hardly uses the word.

For years he taught creative writing and athletics in Macalester College. He has found creative work and athletics to be the best discipline for the growth of the spiritual life. When he first went to the college, the basketball team had a trail of defeats. He called the team together for a talk.

When he got to know the team, he found that there were all kinds of envies, jealousies, and self-seeking ambitions among the men. All wanted to be stars and shine. He told them the story of how Edison made the electric-light bulb. He had first to get all the air out of the bulb, all of it; then to find the filament of fiber or metal that could stand the intense heat. It took time, patience, hard work.

In the same way, Clark said, to have a good team everyone on it must get all the self-seeking personal ambition out of him—every bit of it—and think only of the team. He opened the window and asked them to throw all these feelings out as so much useless ballast. They agreed to do so, some reluctantly.

Then in this new spirit of unit and loyalty to the team,

they drilled as they had never drilled before. The result was that they had a string of victories so sensational that all of them became stars. Other teams wanted to learn the secret. In this way Clark learned and taught what real religion is —faith, self-forgetfulness, loyalty, teamwork, added to skill and good will.

In time he became a wise spiritual leader, applied to other groups these same principles of athletics. He learned that, as William James said, people use only about one fourth of their power. In their spiritual life they use even less—too little to win victory.

Just imagine what the Christian churches could be and do if they had as much teamwork as is needed to win a basketball game. There would be no limit to their influence and power. But alas, they are often divided and weakened by little things of which Jesus said nothing—not one word.

If we want "power to become," we must be ready to work, wait, train, and receive it. As Emerson said, "What you will have, quote God, pay for it and take it." What radiant lives we could live if only we could get ourselves off our hands!

WINGED WORDS

"Your words have kept men on their feet."
Job 4:4 (Moffatt)

WHAT a waste of words!" we may say as we emerge from a church or a lecture hall. Was there ever a race so plagued by oratory? Luncheon speakers slay their thousands with jawbones; radio slays its tens of thousands with similar weapons. If all the words preached in the country on one Sunday were put into books, there wouldn't be enough libraries to contain them. And if there were, some would be constrained to burn them to the ground. Add commencement orations and political harangues to this staggering total, and your head will start to swim.

On second thought, the passion to be assailed by words is not as crazy as it seems. Talk is not cheap if judged by the fees paid to speakers. Why? Some virtue resides in speech, or the checks sent to orators would shrink. The tongue is mightier than the sword. Think of the power of the uttered word! Pointed at an objective, words can start a nation marching. Carefully chosen, they can overturn dynasties. Skillfully used, they can change men's natures. "His words were half battles," said Lord Roseberry of Cromwell. Lincoln's phrases are part of the American language. Churchill's stirring oratory saved Britain. With all their hateful weaknesses, sermons have been known to keep men on their feet.

Observe the negative side of this issue. Why should good people be adept in the use of bad words? Human beings can be very inhuman in their speech. There is such a thing as a traffic in disaster. Newspapers of a certain kind print all the news that is unfitted to keep men on their feet. A ghoulish desire to enjoy bad news makes this business profitable.

Why should so many good folks try to claim credit for piety by a studied pessimism? Even preachers of the evangel fall into a queer habit of propagating gloom. "That God holds you over the pit of hell, much as one holds a spider, or some loathsome insect over the fire, abhors you, and is dreadfully provoked; his wrath toward you burns like fire . . ."—would any man be kept on his feet by this kind of gospel preached by the saintly Jonathan Edwards? In the misguided effort to warn against the dangers of pride, godly souls have knocked men off their feet. "To find a balm for woe" is "angels' work below," but the net result of some angelic souls' efforts is to reduce honest pilgrims to a state of quiet desperation. Constant contact with the Master, who would not quench the dimly burning flame, would improve our vocabulary as well as our manners.

Figure out another queer situation. Eliphaz delivered a home thrust when he chided Job for crumpling under disaster while he had succeeded in putting heart into his fellows by his words of cheer. In plain English, our words carry strong conviction to our friends but they fail to convince us. Let this mystery abide. What counts is not our moods, but the way our words do things to men in desperate plights. Preachers frequently are surprised to learn that what seems to them rather clumsy and inadequate exercises a startling effect in quieting souls about to abandon hope. To put it in another way, we may find our steps being steadied by recollecting what our own faith did to men sinking in the Slough of Despond. God uses weak words to confound and disperse the "powers of darkness grim."

The real value of words may be known by the way men walk as a result of good conversation. It is quite obvious that evil minds can use words to make men frequent questionable paths. Certain areas are forbidden to those who want to walk in the ways of righteousness. When a man is observed climbing the steep and stony path of sacrifice in an unpopular cause, we take knowledge of the kind of voices to which he has been listening. The road of the hard right, taken in devotion to some noble ideal, makes it almost impossible to keep one's feet unless there are words of good cheer spoken by good men.

Above all, when the valley of the shadow of death is traveled by steady feet, when the dearest on earth have passed beyond our sight, we look up and note that Someone has spoken convincingly to a sadly bereft soul. Above all, we listen with bated breath to the words which enable pilgrims to pass through the dark river without breaking their stride. Our Master has acquired a reputation for the way he keeps encouraging his disciples in the last desperate encounter.

"Our people die well," said John Wesley. Could any higher tribute be paid?

David Livingstone came to the parting of the ways. Should he go home to safety or press on into the heart of the Dark Continent, to die in a lonely grave and to end in Westminster Abbey? He opened his well-worn Bible and read, "Lo, I am with you alway, even unto the end of the world." "It is," he wrote, "the word of a gentleman of the most strict and sacred honor. And thereto an end of it." At his word a noble army has ventured neck or nothing. And no one has ever been heard to regret it.

WHAT MANNER OF MEN?

"Should such a man as I flee?" Neh. 6:11

THIS IS NOT a rhetorical question. Any thoughtless answer in the negative would be merely an emotional response and would not settle the issue. For most men danger is something to dodge. Fiction, since the days of the first war, has pictured the ordinary man as the victim of forces over which he has no control. He is to be pitied rather than condemned. Karl Marx propounded the strangely popular theory that economic powers operate fatefully to make history. Some scientific professors of history dogmatically assert that destiny is worked out in terms of trends, and over these man has little or no direction.

Nehemiah therefore seems outmoded. To imagine that a certain kind of man, in peril of his life, will fight and not run away sounds quixotic and unreal. Emerson appears to be a voice from another world when he insists that "an institution is the lengthened shadow of one man." He who runs when trouble comes will not create any shadows.

So we make bold to take Nehemiah's position, though much of the world is on the other side. History is made when good men stand up, speak out, make their wills, and do their duty. The heart of history is the history of its Greathearts.

Since attack constitutes the best defense, let us boldly assault the idea that forces rule and determine fate. A homely illustration will blast this portentous heresy. Trains and trolleys frequently arrive late. Traffic sometimes delays the most punctual workers. But a certain type of person acquires a reputation for lateness. The "late Mr. Smith" gets a name for never arriving on time. Can anyone accept the repeated excuses for his evil habits?

To be honest we must take these forces into account. The sexual drive, while not as absolute as novelists sometimes insist, exercises terrific force. Economic considerations move with fierce insistence. Hungry men will do almost anything to fill their stomachs. Social ambitions operate irresistibly on millions. A bad environment creates problems for good people. Slums make bums. And Christians would do well to make war on decadent neighborhoods. But after the slums have been razed, the main problem cries out for solution. To take a man out of the slums is not to finish the job. To take the slums out of the man is angels' work below. Saints can be found in dark alleys. Scoundrels can be discovered in the choicest suburbs.

Nehemiah gave all he had to the thesis that men matter most. At such a time as the present this point needs emphasis. History is made when a good man battles against the currents of evil and fights his way upstream. Frankensteins create a bomb and the deadly weapon threatens to destroy them. A nation will not be saved by its mighty men, but it can march on to a rendezvous with destiny if it is led by good men.

Churches need to insist on this inexorable law. How shall we judge the church? "By their fruits ye shall know them."

The beauty of its ritual, the splendor of its sanctuaries, the eloquence of its preachers, the social prestige of its membership count for naught unless these produce a climate in which men grow in character. And the state cannot be puffed up about its particular form of government unless it produces goodness. Whatever the ism may be, we shall regard it with respect only if it creates people like Nehemiah, people who stand up and speak out boldly in God's name.

How can it be done? That question causes one to think furiously. A sense of mystery surrounds this issue. Why does the same event reveal some people to be cowards, others to be brave as lions? And the strangest fact is that the reaction astonishes the observer. Stranger still, some so-called strong men weaken at the sight of danger, while some timid souls display quiet fortitude.

In spite of the mystery, one thing does appear to be established. Hopeful became a pilgrim by observing the behavior of Faithful, who perished in the flames of Vanity Fair. Wendell Phillips turned abolitionist when he saw William Lloyd Garrison being dragged by a mob through the Boston streets. John Quincy Adams took up the antislavery cause in Congress because Elijah Lovejoy was killed by proslavery hoodlums. In simple terms, bravery is caught, not taught.

Emerson made a baffling remark on this question: "It is as easy for the strong man to be strong, as it is for the weak to be weak." Our first reaction is to disagree. None of us are naturally brave. It is true, however, as the Sage of Concord goes on to remark, that a man who lives with God cannot easily play the coward's part. When it comes to a choice between God's "well done" and the vulgar mob's approval, it is not too hard to decide. "I can do all things through Christ who strengtheneth me," said a very brave soul. And the saints do not contradict him.

COUNT YOUR BLESSINGS

"He took bread, and gave thanks." Luke 22:19

EVEN IN the shadow of his cross Jesus gave thanks. A tragedy was transfigured into a sacrament, hallowing all the ages. Truly, it is not what happens to us but what we do with it that counts.

Just a loaf of bread, made of wheat grown in any field, ground in any mill, baked in any oven—yet it became the bread of God, feeding millions of hungry human souls. "A Te Deum of the commonplace," John Oxenham called it, turning an hour of parting into a celebration of immortality.

Alas, how far above our low-lying lives, full of aches and ills; above all except the shining ones who follow in his train. How do we know a saint? a wise man asked. By the number of his prayers, the diligence of his charities? No, by the way in which he always gives thanks.

There are those who revel in the adventure of life, grateful for its hardship and hazard—they live, while others whimper and whine. Robert Scott, dying in his tent at the South Pole, wrote in his diary, "How much better has it all been than lounging in too great comfort at home."

One does not have to go to far places to find themes for thanksgiving. Rupert Brooke made an inventory of things for which he was grateful. Each item meant a memory, started a happy thought, brought back a picture, revived a joy. Make your own list while you listen to his: "White plates and cups; wet roofs, beneath the lamplight; the strong crust of friendly bread; radiant rainbows; raindrops in flower cups; the cool kindliness of sheets; the benison of hot water; sleep; footprints on the dew; oak trees; shining horse chestnuts; the blue smoke of wood."

No dull catalogue, but a rosary of memory and beauty—things common to call if we have eyes to see. Yet each has something—the song of a bird at dawn, or a dear and gracious friend, or the laugh of a little child—a joy peculiar to himself, for which to give special thanks.

"Count your blessings" is not just an old saw. It can be a symphony lifting us out of the pettiness of everyday life. It is amazing what our blessings add up to if we take time and pains to make the calculation. It saves us from any sullen mood of remembered griefs and forgotten joys.

An English family, dear friends of mine, had a rule of the home that each was to notify the others of any good fortune. "Just my luck" was the message, meaning good luck—all else forgotten. It was a happy game they played, and it was astonishing to count up the winnings. They looked for good luck, expected it, and found what they were looking for.

Many years ago a dear, ninety-year-old woman preached the best Thanksgiving Day sermon that anyone ever heard, preached it without knowing it. Across the years I can still see her fine face, and hear her voice, telling me in a tremulous whisper a tremendous secret. She would never let me go without saying, "I'm very grateful for all my mercies."

What were her mercies? Food, shelter, a friendly fire, clothing; a few stanch friends, her Bible, which she lived with, a host of memories, the unseen Companion; the joy of a simple faith, tried and tested, and the tranquillity of an unconquerable hope. She was an heiress of God!

She lived in a single room, always clean and tidy. She was not wealthy, but she had found a pearl of great price, more precious than all the gold in all the hills—serenity of heart. She was a tonic for depression, a remedy for cynicism, and a sure cure for the murky blues.

Just a gentle old woman who had lived a sheltered life? Not at all; very far from it. Her story when related—not by her, she never said a word about it—told of sorrow added to sorrow, and many graves along the way. In spite of all, perhaps because of tragedy following fast, blow upon blow, she had learned a certain secret which gave her the victory most worth winning.

She held that it would be better to make every day Thanksgiving Day, and set apart one day as "Grouch Day," when everybody could air his grievances. It would be a dismal day, she said, to those who have no sense of humor; but it would do people good to blow off steam, do their grumbling and have it over with.

How odd that we seldom talk about our blessings, but are always ready to count our knocks; often we remember a week of illness longer than a year of good health. Too many think of their good fortunes as wrung from a reluctant Providence, as if life were hostile and stingy.

It is all wrong at bottom, a wrong slant; our religion ought to save us from such ugly, angular thoughts. Pride is at the root of all ingratitude, the vanity which feels that we do not get what we deserve. Yet we have the love of God, beyond all our deserts, fabulous and forever. Let us give thanks!

THE DOER OF GOOD

"Jesus of Nazareth, . . . who went about doing good."
Acts 10:38

IF WE TAKE the name for the title, the phrase following tells us the whole life of Jesus, its motive, its habit, and its happiness. It is the story of One who in the shortest time did more good than all of us have been able to do.

The story is complete; no word need be added, no word taken away. Jesus lived to do good, only good, always, everywhere, to everybody, in every way. No wonder such a life divided history into before and after.

It was a life of unity and power. It had no dividing loyalties, no selfish interests. The doing of good was his only business. He worked swiftly but he never hurried and never stopped—just doing good to human beings who were lonely, devil-haunted, blind, and hungry.

What is the greatest good that Jesus or anyone else can do to us? Jesus saw with a curiously comforting clarity that the greatest good that he could do to his fellow human beings was to put them right about God—to put them right with God.

If we are wrong about God, or wrong with God, we cannot be right about many other things. Also, if we are right with God, we cannot be wrong about much else that is really important. Like a line of light Jesus' insight went to the bottom of our bungled human business.

Men are wrong about God, they are all wrong with him, therefore they are all wrong among themselves. Their world, which God made so lovely, is a red and blazing hell, horrible and hateful to live in.

We hate one another, we hurt one another, because we are afraid—it is thus that we rob and ruin each other. Once we know that God is, where he is, and how to live with him, life will become great and the world happy. Such was the secret of Jesus—almost too simple to be found out.

As Jesus moved among men in the days of his flesh, they felt the strange simplicity of words and acts, always having one aim, to make God near, real and involved in the life of man as a Friend, a Father. For most of those who saw and heard him, his gospel was too good to be true.

To many today the life of Jesus seems too frail ever to come true amid the shock and thunder of this world. Yet they are haunted by him, whose life was like our own but disinfected of the things which make us hateful to ourselves and others.

There it is—"the human life of God," someone called it—Jesus going about doing good as the one thing needful, being kind to the forlorn, the weary, with an odd tenderness for blind folk and people who are hungry. It makes us wistful to think of him—he was so utterly sure that he was right; and we must be by this time quite sure that something has gone wrong with us.

Take those two little bywords which Jesus used so often. "Cheer up!" he would say to a poor soul bowed low with care or grief—and the load would fall off. He brought new heart and hope to people who had lost both. He was engaged in the great business of cheering people up.

Or take the other little word so often used, "Fear not!" He never lost faith in a human soul, and would not let a man lose faith in himself. He saw people staggering under huge burdens of fear and foreboding, and he wanted to set them free. For where fear ends, there life begins.

Always busy helping someone in trouble, lifting a bit of the load, making the path smoother. Such was his blessed business, and he worked full time at it. How strange that anyone should ever have spoken of him as a Man of Sorrows. He spoke only of his joy. Happy? Yes, because he went about doing good.

Of a statesman of the last generation it was said that he was too much the gentleman to be a man, too sophisticated to be sensible, too learned to be wise. Anyway, our wisecracking civilization is breaking up, it is on the way out. But Jesus, going about doing good, abides and will abide.

As one grows older, one sees quite plainly at first, and then with a devastating lucidity, that sheer goodness is the greatest thing on earth, and that the doing of good is the finest art on earth or in heaven.

Also Jesus was right, utterly right, when he saw nothing worth while, nothing at all in this tiny moment called life—the briefest flicker at its longest—except doing good, just doing good. Even when people argue what precisely is meant by doing good, they know in their hearts, just as we know in our heart of hearts, that only goodness is enduring.

To the young, of course, this will all seem so much sodden sentiment; and so it may seem in our cocksure days when we know more than we ever know again. Just as surely will they learn, if they ever attain to a wisdom that does not crack, that the simple eternal goodness of Jesus is the holiest thing this earth has known, and that to be right with God is the beginning and the end of wisdom.

Life is just an infinitely precious instant when we can see the face of God, if we are truly humble, and it is the face of One going about doing good.

SHABBY LIVING

"The younger son . . . wasted his substance with riotous living." Luke 15:13

THE PARABLES of Jesus show us human life in the raw. He saw clearly, like a candid camera, and his stories are realistic and uncensored.

Not in satire, not with irony, but with vivid clarity he saw the sins, weaknesses, follies, and cruelties of human nature; but he never lost faith in it, never ceased to love it. But he left nothing out of the picture.

Shabby, shoddy living he saw on every side. Shabby means threadbare, worn, ill-kept, ragged clothes and rundown shoes. Shoddy means cloth made of the refuse of old goods, not genuine, a sham—it wears out quickly.

The prodigal son ran wild, had his fling, and then came the pay-off. Sin is always a shabby thing, sloppy and often sordid. The brother who stayed at home was shabby too, respectable but selfish and hard, unbrotherly, sulky, and so cold that one could skate all around him—just plain shoddy.

In the parable of the talents the man who had one talent, instead of trading with it, hid it. "I was afraid," he said, and he let fear sabotage his life. The story might have been told this morning—it is so true to life today. Fear is a racketeer, slimy and shabby, ready to ruin our lives.

Outwardly life has changed much since Jesus walked among men. Inwardly it is the same. A man may dress in broadcloth, his wife may wear furs, yet alas, both may be shabby of mind and shoddy of heart—as much so as the shabby shapes that shuffle along our city streets asking for handouts.

Much of our thinking is shabby, to put it mildly. We think we are thinking, but we are only reshuffling our prejudices. We do not take the time and pains to learn the facts; our minds are shut against new insights. We learn nothing and forget nothing. Who can tell the tragedy of shoddy thinking!

David Grayson, the pen name of Ray Stannard Baker, wrote many books of beauty and wisdom. In one of them he tells of an adventure with a shabby man on a park bench, a down-and-outer. He talked with the man but got no response; he could not strike a spark of fire in him. But he learned two things.

A shabby man is one who takes out of life more than he puts into it. He may sit on a park bench, or ride in a Rolls Royce, but he is a loafer, a dead beat, sponging on the more manful part of mankind. He thinks that the world owes him everything, and that he owes the world nothing.

In other words, he has no sense of indebtedness—none to God for the swift and awful gift of life; none to his country for the great men of the past who made it, often with sorrow and sacrifice. He has no sense of obligation to the future and those who are to come after him on earth.

Such a man takes everything for granted, and complains because it is not better; he takes nothing for gratitude. Washington gave us our free land, Lincoln fought to keep it united and free; the man who does not take off his hat to the great souls of our race is a shabby sort of fellow.

Not long ago the German people voted freely for the first time in sixteen years. We have a right to vote freely all the time, but half of our people do not vote at all. Rottenness may run riot, but many of us do not turn a hand to stop it. We just do not care—we are shabby citizens.

Years ago Dan Brummitt wrote a stinging story called *Shoddy*. It dealt, not with pain, not with pathos, but with church politics chiefly, and it made many people wince and squirm. Civil politics can be shoddy enough, but "sacred" politics are rancid. Some pages read like an inventory of a rummage sale.

Yes, there is a lot of shoddy religion. In the Red Square in Moscow there is a slogan painted in large letters, "Religion Is the Opiate of the People." It is not original with the Russians, even if they do claim to have done and said everything first. No, it was Charles Kingsley, a great golden-hearted preacher, who said it first. Alas, how tragically right he was.

Too much of what is called religion is shoddy, even phony. The great prophets saw that fact ages ago. They saw that a religion of rite and rote puts people to sleep, blinds them to social injustice and cruelty. To Jesus the religious leaders of his day—many of them—were unreal and unholy. He flayed them with blistering words, too cutting for us to use, perhaps.

It is amazing how selfish, how self-centered, we can be in

our religion, seeking safety, not service; seeking to be "let off" for our sins, instead of being redeemed from sin itself. Gandhi said he wanted a religion to cleanse his soul, not merely clean his slate of past sins.

Alas, too many of us are only "honorary Christians"; our religion is not power, but soothing syrup. But who has a right to lecture others about shabby living? We live in glass houses, all of us. It is "the business of God to forgive," said Heine; else there would be no hope for any of us.

LIFE'S LESSONS

"Learn of me." Matt. 11:29

OF THE TWO greatest lessons that life has taught me, the first is the reality of the spiritual world in which we live here and always. In other words, God—not as a mere idea in the mind, a wish, a need, a theory to explain life.

If God is just an idea, when did it come; if he is only a need, why does man need him? Why is there a "God-shaped vacuum" in the human heart? Why, as a great saint said, are our hearts restless until they find rest in him?

The second lesson is the unchangeableness of human nature and the changefulness of human life. No one doubts the second part of that lesson, for change is the unchanging law of life. Life is a flowing river of years, never the same.

But is human nature unchangeable? Of course the spirit and inner attitude of a human life can be altered, else religion would be useless. Yet the qualities, the traits, the faculties of a human being remain the same.

If a man lacks a sense of humor, nobody can give him one. If he has no money sense, as we say, he seems unable to learn any. His temperament can be altered, but only slightly. If he is color-blind, can he ever be changed?

But some of my readers have learned other lessons. One borrows the words of two great teachers, Josiah Royce and Brother Lawrence, to express what life has taught her—a lesson which arms one against adversity.

"Life has taught me that 'the practice of the presence of

God' enables me to endure and triumph over anything that life or death can do to me; I believe that in my heart." To learn to live in God is our only security.

It requires practice, as Brother Lawrence knew, to think of ourselves, our friends, our work, our sorrow, as always in the presence of God. That is the glory of the Bible—everything in it, everybody, is always under the eye of God.

By this simple art one breaks the loneliness of life. Since we cannot go where God is not, there is always companionship, even when we walk in the valley of the shadow, or when we face things far worse than death.

"It may seem strange," another reader says, "while I have been a member of a church since I was a boy, I have been a Christian for only about a year and a half. It was then that I found Christ to be my Saviour.

"The discovery, the greatest I ever made—the simplest, too, when I actually faced the facts—has given me a sense of release, of relief, of peace of heart, and a joy beyond words. If I could tell it, I would do it."

Here surely is a lesson vivid and vital, changing the whole inner attitude of a man, making life a new wonder and adventure. My reader would not give up what he has learned for all the wit and wisdom of all the ages.

"Life has brought me to understand," adds a third reader —an old man—"that I am saved, in the end and in the beginning, not by my faith in God, which may any moment slip and fail, but by his amazing faith in me.

"Whittier has a line, 'By all that he requires of me, I know what he himself must be.' Since he requires me to forgive, to live by the Golden Rule, I know that he too is unfailing in his forgiveness, and lives by the same Golden Rule."

In a most charming letter my reader points out that the whole Bible implies the profound faith of God in the soul of man—its capacity for righteousness, its prophecy, once it learns "the power of an endless life."

"Life teaches every man who he is," said Goethe; but also what he is. By the time a man is forty he ought to know his body and mind, what he can do and cannot do. Time tames us all, teaches us our limits, but also our strength.

"This too shall pass away," was a maxim of an Eastern king, which one reader says has helped him over hard places. "It is a long lane that has no turning," is another way of saying it. Life's changefulness is often full of hope.

If you are weary and perplexed, this too will pass away. Are you happy? Does all that you do turn to success? Beware of vanity, carelessness—this too shall pass.

Caution, consolation, encouragement, and warning are in that old maxim, if we are wise enough to take heed. As Mark Twain said of New England weather, "If you do not like it, wait five minutes; it will change."

Life too shall pass away, and it is a pity to turn its joy into fever, and its fever into fear, and lose its delight and its wonder. Only that which is of value to God will abide.

"Learn of me," said a sweet voice—learn how to live, how to love, how to hope, how to pray, how to give and forgive, how to be blessed and be a blessing.

EVERYBODY'S SAINT

"Provide neither gold, nor silver, . . . nor scrip."
Matt. 10:9-10

FRANCIS OF ASSISI, best beloved of all the saints, a saint of the order of poets, everybody's saint!

How can one speak calmly of Francis? Before one knows it, his words have become a rhapsody—Francis is so fascinating in his personal charm, so fantastic in his happiness, so fearless in his love, so gentle in his power.

As much beloved by skeptics as by believers, he is the saint of the undivided church, a proof of its faith, not by argument but by example; his life at once a poem and a prayer, radiant in his renunciations, gay in his goodness, living the life of Jesus in the Galilee of Italy.

The very thought of "the poor little man of Assisi," so happy in his holiness, evokes even in the most cynical a feeling of wonder, awe, and regret—wonder at the liberty and loveliness of his life, awe at his high heroic purity, and regret that one has so little of his gay and haunting goodness.

Few if any would deny that Francis is the most radiant soul that has lived on earth since Jesus walked in Galilee and Judea. One can no more help loving and praising him than one can help loving surpassing beauty anywhere. He baffles our dull hearts and touches us to tenderness.

Others of his shining company seem to have retreated

into the distance, behind the hills of history; but not so Francis, for he lives in our hearts. He it was who is said to have made the first Christmas "crib"; he it was who wrote Christmas carols, no minor poet publishing his wistfulness abroad, but "God's troubadour."

A poet of exquisite art—artless in his simplicity—an example of piety as rich in pity as it is merry of heart, one of the greatest social remakers of all time, a redeemer of the church from the rot of luxury, no one has more to say to the fat, sleek, fear-haunted materialism of our time.

If union with God is the goal of human life, and all its disciplines are directed to that beatitude, he who achieves that ideal while still wearing our mortal flesh has a strange power over us to rebuke, to command, and to comfort. No wonder he haunts us like soft music and the "Amen" after prayer.

Here was one who, escaping the obsession of selfishness and the prison of pride, reached the liberation of love, and lived in a center of light where malice, suspicion, distrust, petty envy, and pitiful self-glory cast no shadow. Withal he had the saving grace of common sense and the divine gift of humor.

If he was stern with himself—too stern, mayhap, calling his body "Brother Ass," and riding it too hard—he was divinely gentle with others, man and beast and bird. Whereas, too often, alas, we are wont to be stern with others, and tender to our own precious and delightful selves. It is said that he took the words of Jesus literally, but do we even take them seriously?

While praying in a little chapel, he was exhorted by an old Byzantine crucifix, "Go now, Francis, and rebuild my church, which is falling to ruins." At once obedient, he began to gather stones and mortar. Then there burst upon him the full meaning of the command—he himself to be a cornerstone of the church renewed by the faith and spirit of the Master.

Purse and prestige he flung to the winds; wedded to Lady Poverty, he went along the highways of Umbria, his life at once a power, a parable, a prophecy. Such was the exalted spontaniety—acted poetry—which bore his movement forward, as springlike in its gladness as it was exacting in its demands.

Men scoffed then, as now, at such fantastic adventures. But many were thrilled, then as now, by such happy forlornness, such joyous destitution. In an acted parable Francis taught his age, and ours, how rich life can be without any of the things which we think are needed to make life livable.

Thus in an age of fierce feud, brutal violence, vulgar luxury, and fading faith, Francis restored somewhat the lost radiance of our religion; he recaptured the first fine careless rapture of the heroic and happy years when the gospel began its morning march in the world.

"Sweet St. Francis, would that he were here," cried Tennyson, and our hearts echo his wish. Aye, would that he were here to call us back from "thingdom" to the kingdom of heaven, from gaudy extravagance to the great simplicities, from lives decked in silks to hide souls as bare and as poor as a pauper!

How wonderful it is to think of St. Francis, to think of one who, giving up wealth, became incredibly wealthy, and who, in a life like our own but disinfected of the things that make us unhappy, found liberty, peace, and joy.

OLD MAN TROUBLE

"It is good for me that I have been afflicted." Ps. 119:71

In the midst of his trouble the psalmist did not see that it was good. But later he realized that he had learned something from it, and that it was good.

The Bible has much to say about trouble. Said Job: "Man is born unto trouble, as the sparks fly upward." And again, "Man . . . is of few days and full of trouble; . . . he fleeth also as a shadow." Job had every kind of trouble a man can have, but profited by it.

As the book of Hebrews reminds us, our fathers corrected us, chastened us for our good. Shall we not much rather be in the hands of "the Father of spirits"? No correction "for the present seemeth to be joyous, but grievous: nevertheless, afterward it yieldeth the peaceable fruit of righteousness unto them which are exercised thereby."

All through the Bible the point is that our troubles, many or few, are not blows at random. They are not Providence "picking on us," much less hurts of blind fate. If we take them in the right way, they do us good, as they were meant to do. If we had no trouble, we would not know what life is, or what it is for.

A poet speaks of a "ghastly, smooth life, dead of soul," and that would be our lot if it were not for the knocks and shocks of life. The greatest souls have come up through many tribulations, struggles, and troubles without number.

An old, old legend tells of a time when the people of the earth made proud lament, each in his own behalf. Each was full of anger and envy because life had treated him unfairly compared with others. His troubles were too many, more than others had to bear, and they were heavier and harder too.

Each one saw his neighbor walking lightly under his load of care and difficulty, or so it seemed, and it made him unhappy. Every man was sure that if he could trade troubles with his fellow man—all save a few—life would be easier, and he would be more contented. At last something was done about it.

In order to rectify that unjust state of affairs, the gods arranged that on a given day each man should bring his burden to a certain place, cast it on a great pile of burdens, and be rid of it for good. There was one condition, to which no one objected—each man should select for himself another burden, one of the lighter loads he so enviously observed others carrying.

What a day it was! What a pile of discarded luggage! What we would have given to have been there, to throw on the pile our own ache, ill, handicap, pain, our besetting sin, bitter disappointment, or tormenting problem! What a joy to walk away, free at last, bearing a burden of our own choice, not something put upon us without our consent, caused by ourselves or others.

All the world was happy, so the legend goes—but not for long. As each man examined the burden he had chosen, he found it different, heavier, and harder to bear than his old one. Before long every man returned, asking that he be given back his own load again. He knew it, was used to it, and was contented to bear it.

"Crosses for Sale—Cheap," was a sign over a store selling religious objects. If such a sign were put over the door of life, how many customers would it bring in? Few indeed. Yet each has his cross to bear, and how he bears it, with what faith and courage, determines the usefulness and power of his life.

When Ezekiel was sent to his people in captivity, he said, "I sat where they sat, and remained there astonished." He was amazed when he saw the burdens people carried, and the dignity and patience with which they bore them. This also is my humble testimony and tribute, as it is of every minister and rabbi.

Only, in our day new difficulties are added to life. How often someone wants to see a minister or priest. He is hesitant, and finally says, "It is a personal matter." Seldom do people put questions of theology today. In nine cases out of ten it is some domestic riddle, some inward tangle born of a broken home, some personality problem, some inner schism they cannot handle.

The great enemy is fear, but even the old fears—"fear of heaven," or "fear of sin"—are gone. People are afraid of life, afraid of themselves, of failure, of poverty, of illness. Then, too, there are strange fears which are fragments of fancy, having no basis in fact, and these are difficult to deal with.

The loneliness of people is appalling today—so many are insulated by shyness or some other barrier. They are afraid to get into the lives of others, lest they get hurt or humiliated. If only people were more kind, more friendly to one another; it is so easy and acts so instantaneously upon others.

"Let not your heart be troubled, neither let it be afraid," Jesus said to his disciples. He was parting from them, as he and they knew, and he wanted to comfort them. Yet how horribly religion has added to the fear and terror of man, making the face of God dark with anger and vengeance.

Jesus sought to lift this shadow from the human heart—his vision of the love of God was luminous and limitless. Aye, he did more for the troubled heart of man than anyone who has worn our human shape.

AN UNDERSTANDING HEART

"Give therefore thy servant an understanding heart."
I Kings 3:9

LONG AGO a famous poet asked himself the question, "Can anyone in this world be to another all that other could need and desire?" After pondering it all night he answered, "No, he cannot."

No human being, however near and dear to us, can ever be all that we desire. No human relationship, however intimate and tender, can ever be entirely complete and satisfying to us, much as we may wish it to be.

To know that fact and realize it is a part of the wisdom of life; to forget it or to fail to see it may make us miserable. It may make us expect more and demand more of life than life has to give us.

No wife utterly understands her husband, and no husband his wife. In all of us there are nooks, corners, and closets which no human being can enter because we are unable to open them—they are locked.

In one of George Eliot's stories a woman is very unhappy when dying, not because she is dying, but because she knows that her husband can never find the key to the blue closet upstairs—men cannot find things anyway.

Of Phillips Brooks, a great goldenhearted preacher, a friend said that one could get just so close to him. Then a door closed and one heard it click. He could not open it from within, nor his friends from without.

But that is true of every human being, and it ought to be true. We need a "polar privacy," as Emily Dickinson called it, she who was so elusive and so eerie in her aloofness. We do not yet know her secret.

So all through the wisdom books of the Bible, an understanding heart is almost a synonym for wisdom. "Above all things, get understanding," we are told again and again; it is more precious than gold or gems.

To be misunderstood is agony; to be understood is joy. What Chesterton said of the German people is true of many other people: "They lack that little mirror in the mind which enables them to see the point of view of other people."

The prophet Ezekiel went to see the captives who dwelt by the river Chebar. "I sat where they sat, and remained there astonished," he said. That is, he saw what they saw, and was amazed at their heroism and faith.

Astonished? Yes, day in and day out I am astonished at what people face in life, the burdens they bear, the sorrows they meet, the hardships they endure—astonished at their quiet courage and their unsung heroism.

Our soldiers, returning from war, need understanding. No one can be dragged through a jungle of violence and not be wounded in body or in soul, or in both. If they talk, let them talk; if they are silent, respect their silence. It will be difficult for them to refocus their lives after the horrors they have been through. After all, do not treat them as problems; they do not want pity, they want and they need an understanding heart.

For two years I was in a prison a good deal, serving as assistant chaplain of the great gray prison across the river from our seminary. Reading case histories of the men, as I was allowed to do, was heartbreaking.

To learn under what environment they had been brought up, what influences had played upon their lives, what opportunities they had missed, was to understand, in part at least, why they had become what they were.

In the same way, people work together, play together, but when they go to church, each goes a separate way. We do not know, often we do not try to understand, why a rite different from our own may help others.

"Woman is a dark continent," says a French proverb; but so is man—even to himself. The trouble is that we do not know ourselves. "Know thyself" was an old Greek maxim; it is excellent counsel, but who can obey it?

To have an understanding heart is to have a key which unlock doors otherwise closed and barred. Human beings are sensitive and shy; they feel an unsympathetic attitude quickly, and shut up like clams, hiding from us.

Here lies the truth and solace of religion—only God can fully understand us. "He knoweth our frame," the psalmist tells us; he knows us as we may never hope to know ourselves or others, knows our very heartbeats.

It is not pious talk but plain fact that our only lasting

relationship is with God. If we deny him, we are the victims of an unutterable loneliness which deepens with the years, making life as lonely as death.

Let our prayer be for more light, more love, and more understanding; then pity and laughter and joy will walk the common ways of life. Then we shall be astonished at the goodness men hide from us because we do not love them enough.

HOW TO PRAY

"Lord, teach us to pray." Luke 11:1

THE HEART of life, the soul of religion, is prayer. Unless religion and life are one thing, neither is of much value. Prayer is direct contact with the source of our being, its solace and final satisfaction.

Life, said a great poet, is just our chance to learn how to pray. It is the noblest adventure of the soul, the finest of all arts. To learn how to pray is to learn how to live, to discover the meaning of life.

When the disciples of Jesus heard their Master pray, they realized that they did not know the alphabet of that art. Hence their request, and his reply was the brief, grand prayer, so comprehensive in its consecration.

"Can you teach me, show me, how to pray correctly?" someone once wrote me. "On top of my own difficulties, the burden of another soul has been laid upon me, and I want to pray it through to victory. People tell me that I do not pray correctly.

"One religious person said that I ought not to pray about it at all, since God knows already. Another said that I do not pray 'scientifically'—that is, repeat a series of affirmations, and nothing more.

"Still another advised me to pray about my problem just once, then forget about it. Yet the Bible tells me to 'pray without ceasing.' What am I to do? I am not learned in such matters, but my burden is heavy and my need great."

For one thing, our business is not to analyze prayer, but to pray. Also, if one is deeply concerned about another soul, one cannot and ought not to forget about it. Yet one should not worry about it either, wearing out the soul.

There is such a thing as an irreligious solicitude about God, a kind of anxious prayer which defeats itself. Repeating great affirmations, such as saying the twenty-third psalm, is wise and helpful, but why call it "scientific"?

Prayer is not only an impulse, as natural as breathing, but it is also a technique to be mastered. It took Theresa, the Spanish mystic, eighteen years to learn how to pray. We cannot hope to master it in a day or a year.

All of us are "standing in the need of prayer," as an old Negro spiritual tells us. Every day, everywhere, we need prayer. We must learn in our hearts that spirit with Spirit can meet, if we are to know reality and live victoriously.

We must pray for ourselves—assemble our life before God, thinking things through in his presence, confessing our faults, our follies, our sins. It need not be morbid, but it must be honest, candid, no covering up, no holding out.

We must relax, realize, and resolve—unwind our minds, so to speak, untighten our tension; then realize what our life can be if lived by the standard set for us by the love and will of God, and resolve to do it. Not merely a vague resolve to be better and do better, but we must select a specific objective to aim at. Petition, meditation, adoration are all involved; also self-examination, sincerity of soul, talking with God as a Friend, our Father.

This can be done alone, or in a crowd, once we break through the loneliness, the shyness, the fear, the inertia that handicaps us. We may and ought to have an awed fear of God, but we ought never to be afraid of him, who is our hope and our home.

Only God is permanently interesting, eternally lovely, he who is nearer to us than our own souls, upon whom we every moment depend. To learn to live with him, in him, however briefly and dimly, is to know what life is all about.

This is not pious talk; it is just plain sense. It is going to headquarters for instruction and command. For comfort, too, which is more than condolence—comfort is strength, understanding; only God really knows us and understands.

"I have found great comfort in God," wrote Lowell in his old age, when most of his friends were gone. Even our best friend cannot understand us entirely, for we do not understand ourselves. Prayer cancels our appalling loneliness.

Also we must pray for others, especially our enemies or those whom we do not like. If we do, we will not remain their enemies, and in the end they will not continue to be our enemies. We cannot pray for a man and go on hating him.

But praying for another, whether enemy or friend, is something more than to say casually, "God bless So-and So. It is far more. It means to see another life, its strength its weakness, its pitifulness and its beauty, reverently and with imagination.

Then to lift that life up before God in prayer, detain it there, invoking his blessing upon it. Wrote Tennyson:

> More things are wrought by prayer
> Than this world dreams of.

Our prayer for another may mean his healing—and ours.

The highest form of prayer, when by practice we achieve it, is an intense stillness, asking nothing. Listening, that is, not to an echo of our own voice, but to Someone, not ourselves, whom we cannot deny and remain men.

Why pray if we do not know how to listen for the answer? "I will hear what God the Lord will speak," said a wise psalmist. When we have learned to pray aright, we must be listeners in "the place of hearing," like the people of old.

"Lord, teach us to pray," that we may not die without ever having lived.

ABOUT BLIND SPOTS

"Having eyes, see ye not?" Mark 8:18

To SEE clearly is poetry, prophecy, and religion, all in one," said John Ruskin. Some things we see clearly, some dimly, some not at all.

Every man has a blind spot; lucky is he if he has only one. There is a blur in his thinking, a blank hiatus in his vision, of which he may be entirely unaware—he may actually mistake it for wisdom.

With merciful clarity Jesus saw that men do awful things to each other without knowing or seeing what they do. Their deeds are cruel because their minds are dark. If we are to call anybody a hypocrite, let it be ourselves.

Hear Jesus: "Wilt thou say to thy brother, Let me pull out the mote out of thine eye; and, behold, a beam is in thine own eye? Thou hypocrite, first cast out the beam out of thine own eye; and then thou shalt see clearly."

"Forgive them!" Hence his profound prayer on the cross, the wisest and loftiest prayer ever uttered upon earth, "Father, forgive them; for they know not what they do." Men are not as wicked as the things they do; they hurt each other with the blows and blunders of blindness—but the blows hurt just the same.

"With the booty of corrupt politics he built a church, and was buried in the odor of sanctity." The man referred to was a notorious political boss. "The hypocrite," we say. Such an explanation is too simple. Jesus could use the word hypocrite, he who saw into men as one looks into a glass beehive.

Strange astigmatism? No, it was a blind spot. Sir John Bowring wrote the stately hymn, "In the cross of Christ I glory," yet he forced opium on China at the mouth of a cannon. He was sincere in his piety, but he did not see the ghastly gap between his private religion and his public atrocity. There are many like him.

Of a famous financier who built his fortune by bandit methods, one of his best friends said, "He lacks the imagination to see what ruin and misery his policy works in the lives of others." It was a strange astigmatism; he was a go-getter, and as blind as a bat to the interests of others.

Robert Burns prayed:

> Oh wad some power the giftie gie us
> To see oursels as others see us!
> It wad frae monie a blunder free us,
> An' foolish notion.

But others may see us wrong. The egotist inflates himself out of all proportion, and the man with a sense of inferiority deflates himself.

A whole nation can have a blind spot. Germany did, following a fanatical leader through blood and terror to ruin. It would be unbelievable if we did not know it is true. An entire generation may go blind and rush down a steep place into the sea, like the pigs in the gospel story.

There can be blind spots toward God too. Never has there been so much atheism in the world as there is today. It is blatant, boastful, militant—a strange God blindness. Men who live in an enchanted universe, and yet are unable to see even a footprint of the Divine. It is a kind of theophobia; a hatred of God, or the thought of him.

From the eyes of Saul of Tarsus there fell, it is said, "as it were scales," and he saw the beauty and wonder of Jesus, glorified and winsome. A thick darkness had enveloped him, when an ineffable vision awaited him. Who are we to say a word, we who have eyes, but see not the glory of God?

Who can name the blind spots of the world? Years ago Lenin predicted that Germany would arm itself to death, England would expand until it "busted," and the United States would spend and give itself out of existence. Two of his predictions have come true; will the other be fulfilled in due time?

"Where there is no vision, the people perish," the Bible tells us; literally, they become a mob. When every man seeks his own, all lose the things in common. The issue in our country is not capitalism or communism, but democracy—that is, co-operation, fellowship, pulling our weight, and lending a hand.

Yet the disease of democracy is one of the deadly sins, sloth—not laziness, but a slow death by indifference, the feeling that life is futile and not worth while. Men do not want to work, they do not care to vote; they shirk personal responsibility for the common good, and the rest follows.

Even a man with half an eye ought to see that if our technical skill grows, and our moral life lags and falls behind, we are in for trouble, if not the downfall of society as we know it. It is as plain as a pikestaff, as big as an elephant. Yet how few see what is before our eyes.

It is equally true that salvation is not in science, that we must have a moral revival, and that we can have no moral revival without a living religion. At last we are beginning to get our eyes open. Only God sees the world as it is; therefore he loves it and gives himself for it. My stupidity and cruelty must be as puzzling to my fellow man as his blindness is to me. Each of us must look to his own blind spot and pray, again and again, "Lord, that I may receive my sight!"

BELIEVING UNBELIEF

"Lord, I believe; help thou mine unbelief." Mark 9:24

HERE IS a brief prayer, of which there are many in the Bible, wrung from a human heart in agony. It is the prayer of the father of an epileptic boy, whom the disciples could not heal.

Surely no prayer could be more touching in its pathos, or more true to the needs of the human heart. It is a pattern of all prayer in its grave self-abandonment, as well as in the humility of its believing unbelief.

It does not feign faith by hiding doubt, but pours out its perplexity and need in equal measure. The pleading father laid bare his heart, and in the very act lays bare our hearts, linking us in a common fellowship of need.

No one can hear that cry and not feel himself akin to that far-off father in his woe, in his wish to believe, in his bitter trial by the hard facts of life. It is a page from the book of sorrow which blinds us with salty tears.

The lad had been tormented for years, as if some demon were trying to tear him to pieces. Think of the anxiety of those years—the physicians visited, the remedies tried. How many stories of like kind all of us know!

At last the poor man, hearing of Jesus, came to him, not hopeless but unhopeful—ready to do anything for his boy. These are the things that try the faith of man, not intellectual difficulties which may be an alibi of something else.

Always responsive to human need, Jesus accepted the half faith of the father and healed his son. Faith is a mighty force; even a tiny grain of it can do wonders, no matter if it is mixed with bafflement and dismay.

How strange, how troubled is the little heart of man! Love and hate, hope and despair, faith and doubt jostle one another in the multitude of our thoughts. Even the hardest skeptic is often tempted to believe, as the saint is haunted by doubt.

What right have we to believe? Because man was made for faith, and faith alone releases his powers and leads them forth in adventure and conquest. Its warrant is written in the very make-up of his nature, in its needs and demands.

Man does not merely project his thought and faith upon the order of the world, as was a habit of talk years ago. He is a part of that order, as much as pig iron and potash; the laws of his mind and heart are its laws.

As Tolstoi told Gorki, no man can deny the basic faiths of the heart or ignore them without thwarting his own soul, inhibiting its finest impulses, and inflicting dire injury upon his highest nature. A cynic is a sick soul.

By faith we do not mean the dogmas of one church or another—not necessarily—but trust in the reality of God and the trustworthiness of moral and spiritual vision which underlies and outtops all creeds.

What counts are not the many things we try to make ourselves believe, but the few deep, vital things which we cannot deny and remain men—truths as deep as infancy and old age, as deep as love and death and life itself.

By these things men live. Often they live by a faith the lips deny, God knows why, because the deep needs of life override logic. Faith is a part of the sanity as well as the sanctity of life—suppressed faith takes its revenge.

What have we a right to believe? Of one thing we may be sure: our highest faith is not more than the truth, but less. It is a strange vanity which imagines that the human mind can think things too true, too lovely for God to fulfill.

Today men are trying to live a maximum life with a minimum faith, a truncated faith, cut to fit our current fads of thought. It cannot be done. Only a great commanding faith can make men equal to the demands of our time.

"Be not faithless, but believing," Jesus said to Thomas. Dare to trust the highest the mind can think or the heart can hope for, because the highest we can hope for, the highest we can dream or desire, will fall below what God will show.

Life and love, joy and sorrow, pity and pain and death, the laughter of childhood, the coming and going of days, all the old sweet, sad, glad human things that make our life—these are the bases of our faith in God and immortality.

Not argument but insight; not logic but life; not debate but discernment is the path to the truth which makes all other truth true. Pascal was right when he said that the heart has its reasons which the reason does not know.

It is out of the heart that man believes unto righteousness.

As he thinks in his heart, so he is. The real religion of a man is not always what he professes, but what he does—what he lays to heart and acts upon, and thus knows.

If we follow our deepest faith, hold the highest faith we know, even amid the awful facts of life, finally it will hold us. It is always wisest to trust the highest, even if we must often hold to our faith with bleeding hands.

Faith and doubt will play hide-and-seek in our hearts to the end, but if we practice faith, it will grow and gather power, even "the power of an endless life," and make us victors over life, however hard, and not victims of it.

BLESSED MEMORIES

"In remembrance of me." Luke 22:19

A WOMAN asked me to write a few words for those who in middle life find themselves alone in the world, with only their memories of happier times, and who dread the coming of Christmas.

My correspondent wrote on behalf of a group, all of whom consider themselves Christians. Yet because memory brings pictures of Christmas trees, gifts, carols, cakes, parties, churchgoing, but always with someone who is no longer here, she said, "We would like to forget Christmas." But they cannot forget.

Ah, yes. Do not all of us know, as we grow older, what my reader means, men as well as women? Life takes from us those who are the joy of life, leaving us a dull ache of heart, waiting for unreturning feet. The joy of Christmas, so homey and so heavenly, makes our love and loss and longing more acute.

Often one wonders which hurts us more, happy memories or painful memories. The mind tends to throw out unhappy memories, or to cushion them, but lovely and blessed memories haunt and hurt us. Sometimes it is as much as we can bear, bringing back the days that come not back.

These dear women do not sit idle, bemoaning their lot. They are busy helping others who are more unhappy than themselves—more than one takes care of a family in need.

But they cannot be going every moment, and between times there are hours when Christmas seems almost cruel.

Now consider. Dickens has a story, *The Haunted House,* telling of a chemist who was tormented by unhappy memories. As he sat one night by the fire, a spirit appeared and told him that he could relieve him of his distress if he would permit him to take from him his power of memory.

The unhappy man closed with the offer, and became a man who could remember nothing, either good or bad. But so great was his misery, and the misery of others—for he had also been given the power to strip others of their memory—that he besought the spirit to give back his memory.

The story closes with the prayer, "Lord, keep my memory green!" Our problem, then, is to manage our memories, and not let them manage us. It is not easy to do, but it can be done if we have the right attitude. Hear now a true story which has helped me no end, times without number.

In his autobiography Lord Haldane tells how, when he was a young man, for six weeks he was engaged to a beautiful girl. During that six weeks his happiness was absolutely perfect, and he looked forward to years of happiness. Then a very strange thing happened.

Suddenly without warning the woman he adored broke off the engagement. She gave no explanation whatever, and one infers that he never saw her again. He never knew the reason for her act. Fifty years later the only comment he made was, "I was not then, nor have I ever been anything but profoundly grateful to her for that perfect six weeks."

There was no word of blame or bitterness, only gratitude. The glory of that radiant interlude had lived in his heart, a vivid and lovely memory, through all the years. It was his forever; nothing could rob him of it. He was an old man, but there was something young singing in his heart.

This truth is for us—nothing can take from us the beautiful experiences we have had. They are ours eternally if we keep them. Only we can rob ourselves by ingratitude, or forgetfulness, or by letting the fears and cares of today plunder us, leaving us poverty-stricken and forlorn.

"Lord, keep our memory green," we must pray. "Teach our hearts to forget the things we ought not to remember, and to remember the things we ought not to forget. Make us to know that 'those who love God never meet for the last time.' For memory, the mother of faith, hope, and love, we give thanks."

When I was a lad, our pastor preached a sermon which still lives in my heart. His text was the words Jesus said when Lazarus was called back from the dead, "Loose him, and let him go." We must not think of our friends as dead, but as living, growing—else they will be dead indeed to us.

Think of them as alive; then they are free, and so are we. Death has not robbed us. If only we really believed what we say we do. Why let a happy yesterday mar today, or an unhappy today becloud tomorrow? It is not by regretting what cannot be changed, but by using today wisely, that life becomes richer.

It must be that heaven is the place where lost things are found, if we live in remembrance of him who is the gentlest memory of the world. Francis of Assisi "remembered Jesus," when the sunlight fell on the snow, and it "broke his heart." Such beauty bent his knees in prayer.

Life is longer than it looks, deeper than we have fathomed, and there is something in our little, dreaming souls which neither time nor death can touch. "Lord, keep our memories green!"

THE ROAD AHEAD

"I am the way, the truth, and the life." John 14:6

AGES AGO a poet in China wrote, "I want to go back, but there is no road back." That long-dead singer learned a truth we all learn soon or late, a truth which can be sweet or bitter, depending on how we use it.

There is no road back. Our only path lies ahead into the future, and we carry the living past with us, within us. Today the future is dim, hidden, confused—we cannot see our way. The unknown baffles us, terrifies us, making us afraid.

A sentence in a recent letter puts into a few words what is in many hearts, "We want to travel the right road, but we do not know which road is right, and we do not know how to travel together." Here, in a few words, is our plight.

Man has a genius for trying every wrong way before he finds the way to go. Actually he has tried every way, every kind of state, every sort of social order, but they seem to lead only to a dead end. He is now stymied.

One thing at least must be plain to all. Either man must find the path marked out for his soul and follow it with faith, courage, and wisdom, or he is lost. Today he is at the crossroads, and there is but one way to life.

Yet ever at our side, our fellow traveler, is One who knows the way and how to follow it. By the mercy of God we have a light-bringer and way-shower, waiting for man to give up his fear, his suspicion, his hate, and follow him.

"Seek ye first the kingdom of God, and his righteousness; and all these things shall be added unto you." That is, put first things first, seek the reign of God in the hearts and homes of men, and the path of man is plain.

What is the trouble with the world? It has a wrong scale of values. Until it makes an about-face, changes its way of thinking and its plan of action, it can never have peace, harmony, and an ordered and fruitful life.

Yes, there is a divine scale of values, which Jesus stated in his own simple way. The tragedy is that man has turned that scale upside down. His life, his society is like a pyramid tilted on its apex; it cannot stand for long. By contrast, here is the way of Jesus.

First, to love God with all our heart and soul and mind, to put God where he belongs, not an afterthought or a last desperate resort, but first and highest, the source and meaning of all.

Second, to love our fellow men as ourselves, in the same practical, helpful way that we love ourselves, How? By doing unto our neighbor as we would have our neighbor do unto us—the law of reciprocity and human service.

Third, then "all these things," as Jesus put it, will be added unto us. That is, everything in life, food, shelter, clothing, science, art, sport, all the things we need. Then everything falls into its proper place, when first things are put first.

Finally, money, which has its place and value and use, to buy things with which to serve God and man. Jesus put money at the bottom; we put it at the top. But if we put greed above need, we turn the scale of values bottom side up.

The profit motive is right and valid in its place, but if it is made the be-all and end-all, making social gains a mere by-product, it means disaster. Yet that is what we have done, and that is why our social order is chaotic.

Such is the plan of Jesus for the life of man. Of course it will be called impracticable, dreamy, unworkable. But is the present human order practical? Does it work? Twice in a generation it has plunged us into war and woe.

When a plan fails so tragically, it ought to be scrapped. The way of Jesus has never been tried, except by a few great souls and a few small groups. When it has been honestly and daringly tried, it has worked triumphantly.

In a famous preface Bernard Shaw told us that he is no more a Christian than Pontius Pilate. But he added that after studying human affairs for sixty years, he could see no way except the way Jesus would take if he were a man of state.

Here is the real issue before our age. The destruction of mankind is now a possibility, if not a probability, for it is later than we think. Our human society ought not to be allowed to go to wreck without trying the way of Jesus.

Ever he stands offering us the way without which there is no going, the truth without which there is no knowing, and the life that interprets life. To reject his wisdom, to ignore his program, may mean the end of human society.

Surely we have learned that individual religion is not enough. It is precious, but by itself it falls short of our need. We must have a redemptive society—we must live together, and together build a city that will endure.

Ever the road stretches ahead, and we must follow the way and wisdom of Jesus if we are to have life and have it abundantly. Other way there is none; all unwise ways have been tried and they have failed. We must try the way of Jesus.

MOTHER'S DAY

"Behold thy mother." John 19:27

God could not be everywhere, so he made mothers," is an old Hebrew saying.

It puts into words what men and women have always felt, and that is why mother and home are the loveliest words in our language.

"Man builds the house; woman makes the home," is another saying equally true. Such sayings go down to the basis and springs of the best in human life. A society is known by the place it gives to the mother and child.

The home is the first center of society, where begins our struggle against the solitariness and selfishness of life. It is there, in a haven of tenderness and sacrifice, that the highest life of man begins and grows.

The mother who bore us went down into the valley of mystery and pain, not knowing whether she would return. Fear struggled with a thrilling expectancy in her heart—she faced death in order to give us life.

Truly we are bought with a price, and our relation to our mother is unlike any other tie that binds us to human souls.

The infancy of other beings is brief, at longest a few months. The baby bird is pushed out of the nest and made to fly, or fall and die. It is the long infancy of man, his helplessness, which creates the love of mother and father, and makes the home a sanctuary of faith and truth.

If it were not for the brooding beauty of father-mother

love on earth, it is doubtful whether there would be even a gleam of love in heaven. Here is the root of the love that believes all things and endures all things, which never tires, never lets go, whatever adversity of sin may befall us.

No wonder a famous preacher used always to begin his prayers, "Our Father-Mother God." He found in the home, where the Word becomes flesh, the secret and the prophecy of "the love that moves the sun and all the stars above."

Day by day, year by year, by what she is, a mother teaches, stimulates, restrains, inspires. Her influence builds character, sets the pattern of life for her child, and conditions its response to ideals of beauty and truth and goodness in the formative years when impressions are vital and lasting.

"Give us other mothers and I will give you another world," said Augustine, whose mother, Monica, by her good life in an evil age, by her lamp of prayer always burning, saved her son from the temptations of his time.

If there had been no Monica, there would have been no Augustine. She was the mother not only of his body, but of his soul. At last, together, mother and son were caught up into the heavenly vision which sanctified both.

Then, as often happens, the son by his genius gave fame to his mother, else we would have known nothing about her. Again and again a son or a daughter has given lasting renown to a mother who otherwise would have been unknown.

If Lincoln had been killed in the Black Hawk War, if the slavery issue had not been injected anew into politics, or if he had failed, we would know nothing of Nancy Hanks. Even her name would never have been heard.

A madonna of the wilderness, "shrewd, dark, lonesome," her life was broken and her death untimely—but she lived on in the heart of her son, and lives in our hearts. "All that I am I owe to my mother," Lincoln said in reverent homage.

As he sat in the White House reading his Bible, across the years he could hear her voice between the lines—tender, holy, haunting. Behind the man there was always the memory and influence of his mother.

If Whistler had not been a great artist, we would not have the painting of his mother, with her dainty lace cap, her cameo features, her exquisite ways, her hands, old and gentle—folded in her lap, prim, lovely, tender, strong—a vision to bless and exalt us, bringing back memories of days agone.

Today, if we had ears, we could hear a still, sad dirge in the hearts of millions of mothers bereft of sons in a ghastly war—a sob which follows the evening sun around the world. If we could only hear, there would be no more war!

It is a dangerous age. Never have so many evil influences played upon the home, threatening its stability, its security, its sanctity. There are hosts of noble and wise mothers, but they are fighting against heavy odds.

The rush, hurry, and scramble of life are distracting; its laws are relaxed, its ideals dim. The number of broken homes is appalling. The delinquency of youth stems back to the home, where many a brave mother meets defeat.

Nothing can do the blessed work of a good mother and father. It is basic, and if it fails, what can make up the loss? It is fitting, it is beautiful, to have a day set apart in honor of mothers and their unending and divine labors.

WHEN WE ARE OLD

"Even to your old age . . . will I carry you. Isa. 46:4

It is amazing how little the Bible says about old age. There are a few tender touches in the Old Testament; in the New Testament nothing at all.

There is, of course, the great passage in Eccl. 12, which begins, "Remember now thy Creator in the days of thy youth." Then follows the perfect description of the slow decay and final collapse of the body, its "return to the earth as it was," and the spirit "unto God who gave it."

A French proverb says, "Fears of old age disturb us, yet how few attain it." That was true in the old days; great length of life was very rare. Old age was an awful thing in the pagan world; hence the Greek saying, "Whom the gods love die young." How different it is in our day when the race is more kind.

The amazing thing today is the altered attitude of old people toward old age. They do not let down and give up to be old so early. Samuel Johnson felt that he was old at forty. Shakespeare retired at forty-eight. Lincoln wrote of himself as "old and withered" at forty-seven, before he became president.

What to those men was the old age of youth is now the youth of old age. Cicero wrote an essay on old age—wise in many ways—but he died at sixty; he would be regarded as young today. There are more people over sixty-five in the world today than ever before; they are young of spirit, full of zest.

Browning wrote of old age as the best part of life, "the last of life, for which the first was made." If we are a little dubious about his doctrine, we do not fear old age as our fathers did. Many do their best work after sixty-five.

Oddly, there is no really great book about old age. Books about childhood and youth are many and wonderful, but no study of old age has appeared. One story, *All Passion Spent*, by V. Sackville-West, is a gem in the delicacy with which the thoughts and emotions of age are sketched. But, alas, it leaves out the dealings of the soul with God, as so many books in our day do.

While old age may be put off, still it comes at last and must be faced. It has its disadvantages, failing powers, stiff limbs, "the lean and slippered pantaloon," and "sans teeth, sans eyes, sans taste, sans everything." And that includes memory. If only we could manage to forget the things that ought not to be remembered. If age clips the imagination, it also cools the fires of passion and brings serenity.

Old people often have little sense of time. Or rather, they have a different kind of time, as a child has. Time and tempo express the same idea, but the spiritual tempo of age is not that of youth. Really, it might be better for some of us if it were. Youth and age hold different opinions of what is relevant.

Relevant to what? Our ambition, our success in life, or the real business of living? The old have a clearer sense of values than most men of middle life. They see "a landscape instead of separate fields"; life as it is, not as man has marred it by his etiquette, his red tape, and his barbed wire. They have discovered that what we call "realities" are very different from reality.

Akin to this clearer, kinder, wiser view of life—more tolerant and less dogmatic than youth—the tendency of age is to shed day-by-day concerns. It is as if long inured to harness, the soul rebels, kicks over the traces, and enjoys being free.

There are other traits of old age too, such as the passion for veracity, the desire to be loved which is not selfishness, and a beautiful magnanimity. The end time of a life wisely lived can be a benediction, large, gentle, gracious, shedding irrelevancies, rejoicing in a sense of the kinship of things.

Youth is self-centered; it loves cliques, the more exclusive the better. It rarely gives love unless it is returned. Not so age, whose affections, if less turbulent, are less touched with selfish motives. Old men seldom feel, as young men do, that the whole world rests upon their back to be set right.

Youth seeks very high for what is near by. It is as we grow older that the single things reveal their wonder. Tennyson saw the whole mystery of God and man in a tiny flower in a crannied wall. After fifty, our bottle of knowledge is so shaken as to be of one color. Faith is for youth; trust is for old age. "Our old neighbor God," is the attitude of age, and we must love our neighbor as ourselves.

Age is opportunity no less than youth, only in different

dress. Ambition lures youth, avarice pursues age—both must be watched, lest they trip us up. The saddest thing on earth is old age and sin—a crass, crafty, cruel, impure age—worse even than a "set, gray, apathetic end." How to grow old is a fine art.

To keep in age the faith, wonder, and glow of youth, ripened, verified, obeyed—that is real wisdom. May all of us learn to grow old gracefully, graciously; as the sun shines in our faces, may they be bright with faith, hope, and love. At eventide may there be light all around the sky!

WASHINGTON

"Our fathers trusted in thee." Ps. 22:4

As RELIGION has its saints, so patriotism has its heroes. A nation is not simply a business corporation, based upon abstract ideas; it is also a great friendship, built upon great ideals, shared suffering, and sentiment.

Love of country, like love of God, is renewed and deepened by the examples of great men who embodied in fascinating form what else might have become vague. The characters of mighty leaders enshrine our national faith.

"First in war, first in peace, and first in the hearts of his countrymen"—so runs the tribute to Washington; and it remains to this day the most perfect tribute ever uttered in his honor, a Gloria Patri of our national ritual.

No one else ever had or can have the same place in our history that Washington has. Humanly speaking, if it had not been for Washington, his faith, his wisdom, his character, our war for independence might have failed utterly.

Never surely has there ever been a more superb example of the weight and worth of sheer character in any man or any age. What Washington did in behalf of liberty and stability was made possible by what he was—his character.

To me Washington is a mystery; his secret eludes me. He was not an orator, due alike to his temperament and his curiously hollow voice. He did not have personal magnetism; at least one does not feel it in his words or deeds.

Men debate whether Washington was a genius or not. Certainly he did not have that flashing quality of mind which amazes us in Alexander and dazzles us in Napoleon. But he had something far more precious and more rare.

No leader ever had more extraordinary men around him, each in his own right a genius. Marshall and Madison were masters of the law; Hamilton was an adept in finance; Franklin a myriad-minded man; Jefferson richly and variously gifted.

Yet all these men—and others whose names make a rosary of genius—acknowledged the supremacy of Washington, bowed to it, rejoiced in it, followed it. They felt no fear, even when he led where no path was—they trusted him.

All men knew that whoever else might betray his people, or sink into self-seeking, that Washington would never do. The majesty of his character, the solidity of his wisdom, commanded the homage of the makers of our republic.

Maxwell Anderson in his drama *Valley Forge* puts these words into the mouth of Washington when half his army was sick, and many deserting, and there was little food fit to eat. He speaks to his disheartened men:

> What I fight for now is a dream, a mirage, perhaps, something that's never been on this earth since men first worked it with their hands, something that's never existed and will never exist unless we can make it and put it here—the right of freeborn men to govern themselves in their own way. . . .
>
> If you've lost interest in this cause of yours, we've lost our

war, lost it completely, and the men we've left lying on our battle-fields died for nothing whatever—for a dream that came too early, and may never come true.

The men did not leave.

Yet Washington is hard to know, he was so reserved, so unimaginative, so uncommunicative. Those knee breeches, that powdered wig and ruffled shirt, work a peculiar spell—he seems almost to have been a man of another race.

He wrote in the stately ponderous style of his day, in which a love letter reads like a passage from an oration by Edmund Burke. Even his letters to Lafayette, full of tenderness and fun, have to be translated into our more vivid style.

In the same way his diaries are among the dullest of all books, because he records little things of no importance. He counted everything, even the trees on his Mount Vernon estate, but he forgot to jot down that he was elected president!

Yet Washington was richly human, albeit incredibly shy, especially as regards his inner life. If he lost his temper at times, he seldom lost his poise; and if he was often silent, when he did speak, he had something to say.

Of a deeply religious spirit, he spoke of divine Providence, but never, so far as I have been able to discover, did he use the name of Christ in any of his writings, not even in his letters—he would not, of course, in his state papers.

This does not mean what it might easily suggest—far from it. He was a Christian man and churchman, yet there is no record that he ever made his communion. His wife did, but he did not.

No doubt he had his own reasons, and they are no affair of ours. He may not have been symbol-minded. Still, he was both devoted and devout. A man may have the substance of religion without the form—and, alas, it can be the other way around.

It is a pity that Parson Weems in his book, and Stuart in his portrait, have ironed almost every human wrinkle out of a great face, and made it look like a sphinx. A man of force, of hidden fire, of intrepid faith, Washington was the greatest man of his generation, and one of the greatest who ever lived.

TAKE TIME OUT

"Come ye yourselves apart, . . . and rest a while." Mark 6:31

THUS JESUS asked his disciples to take time out. "For there were many coming and going, and they had no leisure so much as to eat." How like our own time with its crowds driving us well-nigh out of our minds.

Life today is keyed to the trinity of hurry, worry, and grind. Our days are tense, our nerves are taut, our lives are hung up and strung up.

Besides, a great world weariness is upon us which we are unable to escape or to resist. All the troubles of mankind pile in upon us. The earth is a hall of mirrors, a loudspeaker whose voice is harsh and rasping. Before we know it, such noise and tension beat us down and wear us out.

Sheer tenseness takes a heavy toll of mind and heart. Much of our doubt, dismay, and lack of poise are just fatigue. Our minds get warped and twisted. We magnify trifles, fly off the handle, sputter, and make wrong judgments.

Yesterday we met a man who cheated us—so all the world is a cheat. Or the sky was gray in our business—so all the world must be gray. Or a man of another race was rude—so that whole race must be wrongheaded. Or a woman driving ahead of us did a foolish thing—so all women are bad drivers.

Our business is difficult and we get jittery; we think that the bottom is about to drop out of everything. No wonder we crack up under such pressures. We are so close to things that we cannot see straight or think clearly. We forget that if the world looks drab and dirty, it is because our windows need cleaning.

It is time to take time out and rest. But how can we do it, tied to the wheel and living in a world where whirl is king?

Let me offer an old bit of technique, a formula tried and tested by wise teachers for ages. It is no trick, no fad, but an art by which we can take time out every day. Ten minutes a day, any time that suits best. Make it a quiet time, alone. Learn to relax, to let go, to let down.

Like every art it is hard at first, but becomes easier by practice if we make up our minds and take time to it. We cannot receive the best things unless we make our minds receptive. It is so with music, poetry, prayer.

"Be still, and know that I am God"—not you—is the wise word of an old psalmist. Then in the pause think quietly of what life is, what it is meant to be. How much larger it is than the little things that vex and upset us. If we try it faithfully, little things will become little, big things will become big.

It is helpful to repeat softly to ourselves great words which we believe and want to realize—the twenty-third psalm, the Lord's Prayer, or a hymn in which some soul found release from tension. Repeat the words positively, not timidly.

Relax, realize, resolve is the formula, and the last is as important as the other two. It is not enough to realize, we must resolve to do the things we ought to do and need to do. It must be not merely wish, but will. It must be a resolve.

Try this simple art honestly; make it a habit and you will never drop it. In religion we call it worship; in psychology it has another name. No matter the name of it provided we use it.

Thus one can take a tiny vacation every day—get away from the grind, iron out wrinkles in our minds, escape from hurry, and return to our task refreshed and renewed.

An hour of worship is taking time out—"rest most active," someone has called it. It is like climbing a mountain where we can see afar. It gives us a new perspective, a better sense of proportion. It shows us our little lives, our job and our joy, in a vast setting; it helps us to get things straight on the inside. How anyone can neglect it is hard to know.

There, in a quiet place of beauty, we gather with fellow souls seeking what we seek. We are not alone. We are together, and the fellowship of folk with needs, hopes, longings like our own lifts us out of our loneliness. Away from the scramble for the means of living, we can think of its meaning, its aim, its goal.

Each praying for all, and all for each, the strength of the many comes to the aid of every one. Our neighbors join with us—aye, and the generations of the past, who were also seekers, come and stand by our side.

Take time out; climb above the fragmentary, the partial, the narrow, the petty. Try to see life steadily and see it whole, and know that life is boundless as we wish our souls to be. Relax, realize, resolve—and be free.

LIFE'S BARGAIN

"What shall a man give in exchange for his soul?"
Mark 8:37

SOULS FOR SALE was the name of a motion picture some years ago. I saw only the sign, I did not have time to see the picture, and I have often wondered what kind of a story it told. It has haunted me for years.

Jesus asked the question pointedly, "What shall it profit a man, if he shall gain the whole world, and lose his own soul?" How much, or how little, will a man take for his soul? What is his price for it? What will he sell it for?

How many famous stories tell how men sold their souls to Satan! Sometimes at the end they were able to break the bargain and escape. Jesus himself, in his temptation, was offered the whole world as the price of his soul.

What is the soul of a man? It is himself at his highest and best, his real self, his capacity for knowing truth, for seeking beauty, for loving goodness and God; his ability to appreciate the noblest, richest things of life.

Can a man lose his soul? Yes, by neglecting it and letting it die, by starving it, by staining it with evil, by choking it with things that strangle it, by feeding it on some one or more of the deadly poisons of the world.

As a matter of profit and loss, what does a man win if he gains the whole world, money, power, fame, all the prizes of life, if he loses his capacity to appraise and enjoy truth, beauty, love? Truly it is a bad bargain.

Not many of us want the whole world; we would not know what to do with it if we had it. Yet often enough men sell their souls for much less, an extra bit of comfort, a little more money, security, flattery, authority.

Often, too, a man loses his soul without knowing it. Slowly or swiftly some secret sin eats it away. His neighbors do not know it, his family may not realize it, but God knows that his soul, made to soar, see, and sing, is lost.

"Conflict" is the word used today for inner tension, schism, which tears the soul to pieces. Hence mental collapse, nervous breakdown, neuroses, and the long list of diseases which debilitate and in the end destroy the soul.

Unless these inner conflicts are cleansed and resolved, we face ruin. We cannot live in a welter of deceit, lies, fraud, insincerity; the soul cannot stand it. Here religion, if we know how to use it, is medicine and meat.

To forgive is to give back. "God will forgive; that is his business," said the poet Heine. Yes, it is; else there would be no hope for any of us. If we lose our soul, God will give it back to us, clean and holy, if we let him.

Here is the very soul of all great religion, a truth which has filled the earth with anthems and hallelujahs. But it is no glib and easy truth; God gives our souls back to us only when we give them to him for keeps.

Also, elsewhere Jesus tells us that if a man seeks to save his soul—to hoard it, keep it to himself—he will lose it. Only when he loses it in something greater than himself, in the service of God and man, does he save it.

Such is the paradox of the highest life; it is not a selfish, safety-first idea or plan. To put it plainly, life is giving, not getting; not self-seeking but self-spending—as we see and revere in all the great lives.

Dante in his great poem *The Divine Comedy* tells us that hell is the place where we get what we want on our own terms—that is what makes it hell. Heaven is the place where we get what we want because we want the right things.

George Frederic Watts has a famous painting, "Sic Transit." It shows the body of a man on a bier with a robe thrown over it—a soft, rich, exquisitely colored robe, so lovely that we want to run our hand over it.

Little things near by tell the story of the man. A sword tells us that he had been a soldier, an ermine robe that he had sat in the halls of state. A book of poetry, half open, tells us that he climbed "the peak of song."

A lyre is there, too, telling us that music set him dreaming—music with its "tales and golden histories of heaven and its mysteries," the most ethereal of all the arts. At the bottom of the picture are the words: "What I spent, I had; what I saved, I lost; what I gave, I have." That is the truth Jesus and all the great teachers teach us—aye, and show us in lives dedicated and devoted to the things that make it worth our time to live.

We cannot take it with us—not gold nor power nor precious stones. In the end we have only what we have given to others—sympathy, understanding, lovingkindness; the rest is as dust and ashes blown away by the winds.

Such is the bargain of life. Only these wistful, winged, seemingly fragile souls, with many moods and hopes and dreams, go with us when the lights of life go out, and philosophies grow dim, and we are face to face with God.

O my soul, remember: forgive and give, seek the truth, serve thy fellow souls and the God of all goodness, whose we are here and forever.

CHRISTMAS MAGIC

"Shepherds . . . keeping watch . . . by night." Luke 2:8

It's my belief that no time of year is quite so full of sweet enchantment as Christmas Eve. Even the glad greetings of Christmas morning can never quite equal the hidden joy of the eve that goes before.

If you would rekindle the dying embers of your faith, stand for a moment on Christmas Eve on some busy corner of a city street and watch the faces that go by. No doubt some of them will be hurried and full of anxiety; but it is anxiety for the happiness of others.

For a brief time that throng is moved by the spirit of giving instead of getting, and though people try to hide the wonder of it, they cannot do it. Half ashamed of their joy, they pretend to be too wise to yield to the spell of an hour that tugs at their hearts with all the pull of playtime.

When they get home, they will slip in a back door and walk softly along the hall, as though hiding some dark treachery. At midnight mothers and fathers will creep upstairs, with elongated bundles under their arms, listening breathlessly at bedroom doors.

It is a time of sheer magic, an hour of poetry amid gray days of press. Staid folk suddenly become stealthy, and there are odd silences and whispered conspiracies in every corner of the house. Old friends look at us with an air of mystery, as if they were hiding some guilty secret.

Even sensible people, touched by some eerie, unearthly spirit, do things divinely foolish—learning, for one day, how silly we often are when we fancy we are wise, and how wise when we fear we are foolish. For on Christmas our gray wisdom does not seem very wise, because it is hard and unhopeful.

For a brief, heavenly moment the clouds are off our souls, lifted by happy winds, and we taste the joy of being free from self, free from fear, and know that life is boundless, as we wish our souls to be. For one holy hour we stand tiptoe to the future, expectant, with no drab dread.

Aye, for a strange, haunting interlude childhood and age meet and mingle in glee; memory blends with hope. For one day, so slow to come, so swift to go, life moves with the lilt and lift of a lyric; we take a vacation from ourselves—the doors swing open and we are free.

One little Child to make a woman cry, and then sing—yet what ineffable truths, what unutterable benedictions and prophecies entered the life of man. "Fear not: for, behold, I bring you good tidings of great joy," comes a voice out of the heart of the world to rebuke our fears and dark forebodings.

It is a scene to sanctify the world, as if to teach us that God enters the life of man by lowly doors, at the end of the way of a wandering star, attended by starry ideals and simple shepherd sentiments. Such beauty bends the knee; such wisdom breaks the heart—and mends it.

The manger, the mother, the Babe, the shepherds, the

angels, the stately magi—these are scenes and sounds we seem to have witnessed and heard, so heavenly and so homey, woven with the holiest memories of the past and the highest hopes of the future, to exalt and to bless.

How we remember our Christmas days agone, those when the home circle was unbroken, and the later ones with their vacant chairs. Yet even when we are alone, there is someone to bless in the name of him who is so great a blessing, someone to remember in the spirit of him who is the gentlest memory of the world.

Why do we live for one day by the law of love, and so soon forget? Why do nations at war lift bloody hands in prayer to One who taught them to love their enemies? Is there any explanation of such a discord? To my thought, yes. Christmas is a prophetic day, looking not so much backward as forward.

It belongs to an order of life not yet attained, to a religion not yet realized, to a coming but distant time which all prophets have foreseen, when man will be ruled by "the better angels of our nature," and justice will reign, and pity and joy will walk the common ways of life.

Welcome the spirit of Christmas, symbol of the Child and "the cradle endlessly rocking." May it flourish to the confounding of all unkindness, all uncleanness. It takes us down from our towering pride, and teaches us humility and a wise charity. It is needed to keep our souls alive.

It brings us back, on one day at last, to a simplicity of faith in the Golden Age, free of the shadow of night and the fear of the morrow. Blessed Christmas day—it gives such as have lost their child heart hope that they will find it again, and become such children as we never yet have been.

All because of one little Child, born ages ago under a singing sky!

ASKING FOR IT

"Ask, and it shall be given you." Matt. 7:7

"He's asking for it," we often hear it said. It does not mean that a man is asking for a thing in so many words, but that he is acting in an unpleasant manner, and that he will get a reply of the same kind. For there are more ways than one of asking for things. Often enough we get what we neither want nor ask for. Then again we sometimes get what we do not want because we asked for it by our attitude and acts.

If a man drives his car carelessly or too fast, we say that he is asking for an accident. If he goes to sleep in his bathing suit, he is asking for a cold; if he eats too much, he is asking for indigestion. Not by word of mouth, to be sure, but just as certainly as if he had put it into words.

In short, our way of living shows what we are asking for in life, whether we realize it or not. Our words, our acts, our spirit come back to us like echoes. If we are critical of people, if our tongue cuts like a knife, if we are envious, jealous, suspicious, we are asking to be let severely alone.

By the same token, if we are generous, thoughtful, unselfish, seeking to serve, we are asking for friends, and we get them. We may not deliberately be trying to make friends, but we make them as a kind of by-product of our gallant and cheerful way of living—as two and two make four.

The real question, then, is what are we asking for in life?

What do we really want? Do we know? We may know what we want to have, what we want to do. But do we know, have we actually decided, what we want to be?

In other words, what are we praying for? Our real desire in life is our life prayer, and we must be careful what it is, because in the end our life prayer is answered. Our character is the sum of our desires; we become what we ask for —our life prayer organizes our energies and our days.

How strange it is! Few people ever actually ask themselves what they want to be in life. Or if they sometimes toy with the question, they do not take the trouble to answer it clearly in their minds. They just drift through their days, taking it for granted that everything will come out somehow.

If we put as much brains into the business of living as we do into our business, how much better things would be on the inside. We would take ourselves in hand, have a purpose, an objective, and a plan. There would be no more coasting, no more just living at random, but discipline and direction.

A friend told me how he had to run to catch a late bus. He almost missed it. Half out of breath, he sat down; there was no one else in the bus except the driver. Suddenly he began to think and wonder. He asked himself some questions he had never asked before. Had he really caught the bus?

"The real bus," he explained, "the bus marked with the word 'Life' on the side, and 'Happiness' on the front. If not, where and why had I missed it? Before I knew it, I was on the spot, and it was not a happy spot either. In a queer way there was no way to get off the spot. I had to face myself."

As the bus glided along, he took stock of his situation. He had good health, a good job, a good home, and money enough to provide his family with the necessities, and a few luxuries. He worked eight or ten hours a day and played a fair round of golf betweenwhiles. He had many friends.

Yet something was missing. He got no real kick out of life, because he found no real purpose in it beyond the daily grind, the plotting and planning and struggling and saving to get along and keep ahead.

Inside those limits he had achieved security, and like the rest of us, he was afraid of insecurity. But, alas, he suddenly realized that the limits were too narrow, and his purpose was no real purpose at all. He had made an end of something which is really only a means to an end.

"My life has been carefully filled with the things that preserve it," he said to himself, "but I have never asked until now why I was preserving it. What is my life for? What have I done with it? Have I ever really lived? I have spent my days stringing the fiddle, but have never played a tune on it."

There are people like my friend. I talk with them day by day. They have everything to make them happy—except happiness. They have security, but down inside they are very insecure about life itself.

Yes, my friend asked for it. He set too narrow a limit to his life. It is not too late for him to give himself a something far greater than himself, asking no reward—to get himself out of himself and off his hands.

If we would have more of life, we must ask for it. Up until thirty life comes to us; after thirty we must go to it, take hold of it, handle it, dare its risks, and by the grace of God make it too great to die.

LET'S FORGET

"Forgetting those things which are behind." Phil. 3:13

AN OLD mystic offered a wise prayer, "Lord, help us to remember the things we ought not to forget, and to forget the things we ought not to remember."

Memory is a mystery. At times it acts like a crazy witch; it keeps bits of rags and straw, and throws away jewels. It has holes in it through which many things drop out which ought to be kept and treasured.

But there is method in its madness. If we did not forget, if we recollected everything all the time, life would be clogged and choked. The past would rush in upon us, overwhelm us, and sweep us utterly away.

Often in an hour of crisis a delicate barrier in the mind gives way, and memories, like the waves of the sea, come rolling in, flooding our hearts. For the moment we have lost the power to hold back the tide, and like the psalmist we cry, "All thy waves and thy billows have gone over me."

Can we manage memory? Can we sort out our memories, throwing away things we ought to forget, and keeping the things that are precious? Yes, by practice, and still more, by the grace of God. If at times memory needs refreshing, at other times it needs a house cleaning, and the rubbish cleared out.

First, it is no good hoarding injuries and irritations. They ought to be swept out of mind, along with a lot of unimportant unpleasantnesses, about which we make too much ado. They are not worth keeping; we may only aggravate them by remembering them—they make us unhappy, and others too.

If they sting like bees, they need not stick like burs. By brooding over them a spark is fanned into a flame, and "behold, how great a matter a little fire kindleth." In that fire it is our own furniture that is burned up. Very precious things are ruined by keeping old grudges, resentments, and vexations in mind.

Let's forget them, throw them in the ash can, have done with them. They keep us ruffled and feverish; they fill the chambers of the soul with heaviness, ugliness, and gloom. They shut out the sunlight and sour the feast of life. Order them out of the house, slam the door, let them be gone!

In the same way, our sins are the least interesting things about us. If we repent of them, confess them, and abandon them, we may be sure they are forgiven. Why unfit ourselves for a new life by rehearsing them in memory? If we have injured others, we must make amends, so far as possible, but we do nobody any good by brooding over blunders. Why dig up a past that is dead?

As the wise old Bible tells us, "where sin abounded, grace did much more abound," and we may not only be clean, but free. There ought to be no room in our memories for the shadow of forgiven sin. "His banner over us is love," and that banner waves over all our yesterdays and our tomorrows.

Our good deeds, too, ought to be done on the sly, then

forgotten. We are not to let our right hand know what our left hand does, much less always be telling everybody about it. "Take heed that you do not your alms before men, to be seen of them," and we may surely add, "nor to be seen of self," lest by gloating over our goodness, even to ourselves, we spoil the beauty and joy of it.

A defective memory may be annoying at times, but it is a blessed thing if we contrive to forget our attainments. If we linger over a success, we are apt to become self-satisfied, and have no energy for anything beyond. To rest on our laurels is to put an end to growth, and come to a period in life.

As someone has said, if we sit down and fondle a victory, we may lose the campaign; our success may drug us into defeat. Many a man is ruined by too much remembering—by living over the past, and finally going back and living in it. Behind us the closed gate, before us the open road!

It is said that when Thorvaldsen finished his famous statue of the Christ, he sat down and wept. For the first time in his life he was satisfied with a piece of work. He knew that his genius had burned out. He had lost the vision and allurement of things more lovely yet to be realized.

Yes, "forgetting those things which are behind" is the first part of wisdom, but Paul adds, "and reaching forth unto those things which are before." For the glory of life is the glory of going on and still to be. There is still work to do, love to win, and beauty passes with the sun on her wings.

Today, tomorrow, and to the end there are some things

we must never for a moment forget. As we read in the glorious Ps. 103, every day, everywhere, and always, we must remember God, who is the health and hope of our hearts. "Bless the Lord, O my soul, and forget not all his benefits: who forgiveth all thine iniquities; who healeth all thy diseases; who redeemeth thy life from destruction; who crowneth thee with lovingkindness and tender mercies."

Then follows a shining list of the things we ought to remember, and remembering, teach our hearts a hymn of thanksgiving and praise.

THOSE GONE BEFORE

"He took bread, and blessed it, and brake, and gave to them."
Luke 24:30

As THESE words were written, a message came telling me that a few hours before my only brother passed softly, and not without warning, to where beyond these shadows there is light.

Did he, when he awoke from the shadow of life, know our little mother, who went away many years ago? Perhaps not at first, since even life often changes our friends and we do not at once recognize the old face in the new. Death and growth may alter them still more.

Often life changes us beyond knowledge. When Ulysses returned from his long wanderings, neither his wife nor his son knew him. He was known only by his dog, Argus, and later by his old nurse. His mother might have known the bronzed and bearded figure at the door.

The disciples of Jesus did not know their risen Master at first, when he walked with them in the gloaming, or greeted them by the lakeside at dawn. Gradually they knew him by a tone of voice, a gesture in the breaking of bread, in the little ways that we identify people.

A lovely Dickens story tells of an old woman sitting by a grave, talking to a child about her buried lover. Timidly the child asks her if her lover was an old man. She takes from her bosom a locket and shows the child pictures of herself and her lover, radiant in youth.

"There we are," she says softly. "Would you take that smiling girl for the old woman at your side?" The tell-tale eyes of the child give the answer. "No, no, there is no trace of the girl he loved left in me. He would not know me and he is as young as ever," she sobbed.

But there she was in error, as we so often are. She was thinking of her lover as he was years gone by, just as we think of our friends as they were when they went away. Life is growth, unfoldment, and while our friends gone before may not grow old as we do, life changes them.

Even here, often we know our friends when we see them in the perspective of death better than when they were with us. Alas, we are too close to them to see them truly. Tennyson knew Arthur Hallam better when he saw him in the whiter light of the unseen, just as we know Lincoln today as no one knew him when he struggled amid the shadows of war.

"Loose him and let him go," Jesus said of Lazarus when he called him back from the grave. That is, let him go, let him grow, do not keep him wrapped in grave clothes. If we think of our friends as dead, they will be dead to us. It is a pity when we let the dead die in our hearts.

No, let us think of our loved ones as living, growing, going on, and still to be. Life is movement and mutation; it is a river of years, and we cannot bathe twice in the same waters. It is memories and dreams; it can be the victory of faith and the tranquillity of a great hope.

In one of the Drumstochty stories Margaret Howe, "who was nearer to the heart of things than anybody in the glen," said to Lily Grant, "Dinna be ashamed of your dreams, Lily; they'll come true some day, for we cannot think better than God will dae." There speaks the heart of a wise faith, and faith is not just feeling, not yielding—it is a force.

Here is both the basis and crown of all our faith, here and hereafter—faith in the love of God, the mightiest and gentlest power in the universe. It is the only force that cannot be defeated; it "believeth all things, hopeth all things, endureth all things."

The text of my first sermon was the anthem of Paul in which he said, "I am persuaded, that neither death, nor life, . . . nor things present, nor things to come, nor height, nor depth, nor any other creature, shall be able to separate us from the love of God."

This is the victory, in life and in death, and all that lies between and beyond, even our faith in the love of God. This is all my religion, all that I need, giving me help for today, and hope for the morrow. Never have I been tempted to imagine—in my vanity—that I can think thoughts too high or dream dreams too lovely for the love of God to fulfill.

In his great hand we stand here and always, and no one can ever fall out of his hand. There is time enough and space enough and power enough for all blunders to be made right. Even the death of a little child may mean that heaven must have little ones, and so not be less blessed.

Yes, because God is love, almighty and unforgetting, I rest content in my sorrow and loss, knowing, as Whittier wrote:

> Life is ever lord of Death
> And Love can never lose its own.

LET'S BE TOLERANT

"He that is not against us is for us." Luke 9:50

TWICE IN this chapter Jesus rebukes his disciples for being petty of mind and intolerant of spirit. "We saw one casting out devils in thy name; and we forbade him, because he followeth not with us," they said. Jesus was astonished and said, "Forbid him not: for he that is not against us is for us." In other words, all the doers of good are allies. But his disciples wanted all good work done with them, in their way.

Again, as Jesus passed through a village of Samaria, the people were not cordial to him, such was the ill-feeling between two races. "Lord, wilt thou that we command fire to come down from heaven and consume them?" Jesus replied: "Ye know not what manner of spirit ye are of. For the Son of man is not come to destroy men's lives, but to save them."

Such bitter, vindictive spirit must have shocked Jesus—but, alas, it is still with us.

"We are the people, we have a corner on truth, our way is the only way. Those who think and do otherwise are wrong and evil." This spirit has filled the world with endless feud, misery, bloodshed, horror, and sorrow.

Intolerance! How ghastly it is and what a terrible history it has! How slowly men learn to live and let live. They want to impose their ideas upon others, as if they were infallible.

Of course if what we tolerate is good, then we should not just tolerate it. We ought to back it up. If it is wrong and evil, then we ought to detest it and seek to destroy it.

Such is the case against tolerance. Tolerance is not a blanket sort of thing; all depends on the spirit from which it springs. Some forms of tolerance ought not to be tolerated.

If we tolerate a thing because we are indifferent, it is not tolerance—it is inertia. We do not care, and do not want to be bothered—we might have to do something about it. Such tolerance is just a dodge.

Or a man may be tolerant because he is a skeptic, and thinks one idea is as good, or as bad, as another. "What is truth?" asked Pilate, but he did not stay to hear the answer. Nor would he have understood Jesus.

Often tolerance is a mere expedient, using the tolerance of others to undermine and destroy all tolerance. Shall we tolerate such mock tolerance? Yes, but we ought to see the thing for what it is, and see it clearly.

What we need to fear is not freedom of thought, but freedom from thought. "When a man's ideas are too strong for you, strike at his skull," said Stalin. But violence is a sign of weakness, a sign that we have run out of ideas.

Voltaire said, "I do not agree with a word that you say, but I will defend to the death your right to say it." If we tolerate only those who agree with us, are we tolerant?

All these kinds of tolerance are defective; they do not go deep enough. Any true tolerance must rest upon humility, and the wisdom that sees that other people have ideas and feelings and loyalties which deserve to be considered and consulted. After all, they might be right, or partly right.

Surely it is truth that we want, and it is vanity to think

that we have all the truth. If another man has a truth, we want to know it and make it our own. We must respect him, try to understand him, not merely tolerate him.

The gospel of Jesus was met with intolerance, even frightful persecution. It was held by the Roman Empire to be a subversive, dangerous teaching. Yet it lived, and finally saved civilization when the empire went down.

Many new ideas meet opposition, anger, and intolerance, and must win their way. Toleration for the sake of toleration is not enough; it must be for the sake of truth. It asks us to be sportsmen, humbly seeking to find what is true.

It asks for the will to study other peoples and faiths, and the patience to appreciate truth in garbs other than our own, free of selfish pride, and in reverence for the truth.

As someone has said, without this spirit "tolerance is an unlit lamp." Unless it has its roots in a sense of the common sonship of man, and his spiritual well-being, it fails of the very goal which it should aim at.

For tolerance exists not to rule, or merely to yield, but to serve by intelligence and good will to discover the truth that makes us free, equally from bigotry and blindness, and—most of all—free from the petty spirit.

Let's be tolerant in faith and fellowship, knowing that truth is greater than our little minds and that all those who seek the truth are friends. Each needs the insight, experience, and daring adventure of the other.

In anger and hatred we lose the truth; in love we find it. For to know the highest truth we must be truehearted.

I WASH MY HANDS

"Pilate . . . took water, and washed his hands before the multitude." Matt. 27:24

WHAT a scene! It is so typical of the efforts of people to get out from under, to "pass the buck," as we say in everyday talk. How many men try to evade their duty and responsibility, try to escape.

Jesus was a prisoner before Pilate, governor of the province. Pilate, after examining his prisoner, decided that he did not deserve death. One often wonders what the words of Jesus mean to a man like Pilate.

"My kingdom is not of this world," said Jesus. How would such words strike a hard-minded military man like Pilate? No doubt he would look at his prisoner, wondering whether he was not just a poor harmless visionary.

But Pilate was a politician. He had to think about his job and how to keep it. The fury of the mob was relentless. So he washed his hands saying, "I am innocent of the blood of this just person: see ye to it."

How strange it is! Many of the Caesars are forgotten, yet the name of Pilate, a petty Roman officer, is repeated in the creed of the church by millions of people every week. What an unenviable, undeserved immortality!

To play politics with the life of Jesus, sending him to his Cross when Pilate knew that he was innocent—this is the limit of tragedy, absurdity, and self-seeking; a man of power failed to use it justly in face of the facts.

But there are many excellent people who are ready to give of their best in the way of help and advice, either to individuals or to causes, so long as their ways of thinking and doing are adopted by those they seek to help. Otherwise they "wash their hands" of them. That is a terrible thing to do—to stop helping unless it is done in our way. Parents do it of their children. "If you don't listen to us, you can go your own way; we are done."

How many outside the church say, "The church has gone wrong; the most disturbing thing about the church is that it is not disturbed about anything. I wash my hands of it." How easy for disillusioned folk to say that.

At the end of World War I our country did just that thing in regard to the rest of the world. We were disgusted; we tried to resign from humanity. "Let Europe stew in its own juice," we said angrily.

But it did not work. It was the easy way, but we were never meant to take the easy way. There is no easy way to the great goals of humanity. To reach them requires time, patience, tact, humility, and faith.

So whether it is the human family, or members of our own family, when we have given our advice, and know it is right—that is very important—and that to ignore it means disaster, still we must not sulk and refuse to help.

No matter; they will know it in time too. In their hearts they will know that we who advised them wisely once can help them again. Shall we refuse to do this? Certainly not, unless we think more of our way than of those who need help.

For years Winston Churchill, in speech after speech, pointed out what was going on in Europe, and told what such things would lead to. Nobody would listen. What he said came true, yet not once did he say, "I told you so."

In churches, in clubs, in all sorts of groups there are men and women whose advice and influence are of the first importance. But they have resigned because their counsel and service have not been accepted.

As for responsibility, we have today a kind of cult of irresponsibility. People will not face facts, much less pull their own weight. This attitude is fatal to many of the finest things we seek and hope and work for.

Someone called World War II "an unnecessary necessity," but that does not make sense. Yet amazingly all leaders and peoples disclaim responsibility for it. Nobody was to blame. Apparently it just happened on its own accord. By a kind of fatalism it had to come, and so it came. If that is true, a third world war will come in due time if everybody denies any responsibility in the matter.

A famous man, asked what most obstructs the making of peace, replied, "The small-scale, stick-in-the-mud individual." In the last analysis our hopes for peace and an ordered world rest upon individuals—upon you and me.

We—and such as we—are the final source of power and

direction, and the spiritual forces to save the world will radiate from us, or not at all. We are masters of our own fate, if we so will it, and only if we will it.

It is in vain that we "wash our hands" of the matter, and leave it to the politicians to play games. The very existence of democracy rests upon the spiritual quality and intelligence of the individual. It is his job.

For inspiration and example we may look at Jesus, whose teachings the world has ceaselessly ignored. But, thank God, he has not washed his hands of us; he is with us always, even to the end. He does not walk out on us!

HOW TO DEAL WITH TIME

"Redeeming the time, because the days are evil." Eph. 5:16

ON THE last day of the year we gather in the Inn of Year's End, looking back over the year gone by. Many memories, thoughts, and struggling hopes throng our hearts.

There is much congratulation upon so much of the journey safely done, and much well-wishing for the unknown way that lies ahead. Also, there is a mingling of courage and complaint—folks telling aches, ills, and upsets. Those who are brave and have faith agree with Meredith that life is a trust, loaned to us "to do a mighty labor."

After all, wrote Michael Fairless in that golden book *The Roadmender,* what do we ask of life here or indeed hereafter, but leave to serve, to love, to commune with our fellow men and with ourselves, and from the lap of earth to look up into the face of God? Godspeed to the next milestone—and beyond!

How to deal with time—how to be victors over it, not victims of it—is the real question of life. If we let time have its way, it will do awful things to us. It will write wrinkles in our faces, scribble crow's feet about our eyes, and turn our hair from black to white; it will shrivel our souls.

For most of us, Father Time is not a friend but a master, a tyrant. We are under his heel; he drives us, he drags us, he dominates us. We are always in a hurry, trying our best to keep up with him. We must learn how to use time, to master it, to turn it into life—that is the finest secret of life.

Time is life. It is the corrector of errors, the tester of truth, the healer of sorrow, the wisest philosopher, the one preacher to whom all must listen, since it tells us the truth that old people have tried in vain to teach us. Each of us has all the time there is, one moment, one day. We must learn to use it.

"So teach us to number our days, that we may apply our hearts unto wisdom," is a great Bible prayer. We must not live at haphazard, but to some purpose, with some method, and so attain to the wisdom that is victory. A true rule of the moral life is—next to God—to respect time and wisely employ it.

By the mystery of memory, that strange time-binding power of the soul, we master the past. Without memory life would be chaos, lacking unity, sequence, and meaning. Memory is the mother of faith and hope. A noble hymn affirms:

> So long thy power hath blessed me, sure it still
> Will lead me on.

Faith triumphs over the present no matter what its ills may be. Duty done defeats the despotism of time, investing its flying hours with worth and meaning. Love fills the vacuity of time with shapes of beauty, peoples it with images of truth, making it green and fruitful and gracious.

In her lovely story *The Little Locksmith* Katherine Hathway tells of a tiny girl who, because of an accident, had to be strapped to her bed for years to keep her from being a hunchback. Denied the joys of other children, she could only gaze out of the window at the tulip tree, or cut paper dolls.

Thrown back upon itself, her mind discovered a magic all her own for the "transformation of detested things into lovely." She saw most people throwing away so many things they do not like. "They throw away experiences, people, marriages, situations, all sorts of things because they do not like them, which by simple magic could be transformed into the opposite."

It is an ugly world in which we live just now, and we are more than a little strapped down. To turn cynical and sour is to admit defeat and failure. How much better if we can find the magic of transforming ugly, undesirable things into lovely things, as all the masters of the spiritual life have taught us.

If faith, duty, and love triumph over the present, hope outruns time, even at its swiftest, leading the way to the city of God, where time shall be no more. For time is only a tiny measured part of that eternity in which we live now and always. With God a thousand years are "as one day." He knows a secret we have not guessed.

Is time the thief, the robber, the tyrant Shakespeare told us about in his sonnets? No, time is our friend if we master it, instead of letting it master us. How can we triumph over time? By living for things eternal, which time cannot tarnish nor death take away. If we live for things that cannot die, we are free!

Here is what Jesus meant by the eternal life of which he

spoke so often. It is not life beyond time and death, but life here and now lived—as he lived—for the things that never wither, never fade, never go out of date. Caesar and his empire are gone long ago, but Jesus lives despite ages of time.

What a life was that of Louis Pasteur, one of the saints of science, whose story stirs us like a drumbeat. He won victory over time by faith in God, by the calm assurance "that the power for good given us in this world will be continued beyond it." Such faith is undefeatable, if we are loyal to it.

At long last we shall learn that our religion, if we trust it and know how to use it, will make us victors over anything that life or death can do to us. For the rest, in the New Year, hope much, fear not at all. If you meet sorrow, bear it; if you find joy, share it; and love God and man with all your heart.

OUR DIVIDED WORLD

"If a house be divided against itself, that house cannot stand."
Mark 3:25

LINCOLN USED the words of Jesus as a kind of text for a famous speech when our country was a house divided against itself. "This nation cannot stand half slave and half free," he said fatefully.

Today in spite of the warm and generous words of Wendell Willkie in his book *One World,* we find ourselves in a divided world. The cleavage is clear-cut and goes down to the roots of our life.

There are two ways of life, two interpretations of the meaning of life, two estimates of the value of human beings, two ideas of the nature and function of the state, and no one can see how they can be reconciled.

If one is true, the other is false. There can be no compromise. If they are to live together on the same earth, it must be in distant and diplomatic aloofness; and even then they are sure to clash if they touch at any point.

In the Russian constitution we read the words, written no doubt by Stalin himself, "There are two theories: to every man according to his needs, that is communism; to every man according to the value of his work, that is socialism. We choose the second." Between the lines a bitter bloody conflict raged.

Trotsky, Kamenev, Zinoviev were communists. They held

by the first theory. But they were "liquidated," if one may use the dialect of the devil, which came into vogue during World War II. In plain words, they were killed.

The Russian system, then, is not technically communism, but totalitarian state socialism. The socialism of England is democratic, with no such idea of the meaning and functions of the state as obtains in Russia.

By totalitarianism we mean the total control of the people by the state: control of their thought as far as possible—all sources of information—control of their life in detail; control of elections, with only one ticket to vote.

By contrast we read the words of Lincoln in a message to Congress:

> This is essentially a people's contest. It is a struggle for maintaining in the world that form and substance of government whose leading object is to elevate the condition of men—to lift artificial weights from their shoulders, to clear the paths of laudable pursuits for all, to afford an unfettered chance for all in the race of life.

Such is our ideal and goal, and if we have not reached it completely, it means much to strive toward it.

Not to crush man, but to turn his face toward the light; to set free his powers of thought and achievement, giving him the joy of seeking the great freedoms of the mind, and to worship God in the way his heart loves best.

These two ideas—ways of living and thinking—divide the world. It is the old fight between liberty and slavery, of democracy and despotism. As Lincoln said of our nation, the world cannot exist half slave and half free.

So lies a sick world in the arms of God. What can be done? Obviously a divided church cannot do much for a divided world. It cannot hold itself together, much less deal with forces at once so cynical and sinister.

Other religions are chiefly racial, but underneath the many forms of our religion there are two kinds, sacramental Christianity and evangelical Christianity. At heart they are one, if they only discover their unity.

It so happens that I have belonged to both, and know both from the inside. There is no contradiction, and where we have two such good things, it is wise to choose both. The more interpretations we have, the richer we are.

But even a united Christianity is not equal to the need of a day when we fear for the existence of civilization, if not for the survival of the race.

No, there must be a rebirth of the soul of man, the advance of the race to a higher level. Man is ready for it, by the sheer bankruptcy of his present plight. Always what seems to be the end of man has been a new beginning.

It will be so again. No one can tell what form it will take, but it will come; a greater humanity with a nobler religion will appear out of the tragedy and the terror and the desolation of today.

EVERYBODY'S CROSS

"If any man will come after me, let him . . . take up his cross daily, and follow me." Luke 9:23

To EVERY man, no matter what his faith, must come a sense of awe when, in the closing days of Lent, the whole Christian world turns its eyes toward a dark cross standing stark outside a city gate long ago.

What can that cross, however heroic its victim, mean to us who live in a distant and different age? Is it a kind of holy memory, kept alive in the hearts of men for centuries, or has it a strange power of its own?

The cross is one of the oldest symbols of man, almost as old as man. When man climbed up out of the dark, he had a cross in his hand. Where he got it and what he meant by it, he did not know—but he held to it.

Older than our era, in Egypt, in the Valley of the Kings, the cross enclosed within a circle was the symbol of eternal life, since a circle has neither beginning nor end. Hence the cross was the scepter of the Lord of the dead who do not die.

So it is as far back as human records run. The cross is the symbol of the clash and collision in life, its fateful frustration which makes it a struggle, an agony. Since this struggle is universal, the symbol is universal.

Two pieces of wood laid athwart each other, the cross stands for the paradox of life; it is rooted deep in the nature of things. It is both a token and a trophy of the mystery of life and its meaning and prophecy.

Every man, every woman, has some mystery in their lives, something that hurts beyond words. There is a skeleton in every closet, a thing hateful and horrible; we cannot imagine why it should have befallen us.

Late or soon, as surely as suns rise and set, in one form or another, each of us will face his own cross. In nine cases out of ten it is made out of a tree grown in our back yard—but it is not always so.

Sometimes it is shaped in part by others; but more often we shape it with our own hands, roughhew it how we will. But there it is, perhaps at the next turn of the road. Whether we bear it bravely, or sink under it, depends on us.

It is the deep fact of frustration and need which turns the eyes of millions toward that high triumphant cross outside the gate. Jesus did not simply tell us the way of life and victory; he showed us the way, step by step.

All his life was a journey to his cross; his days were timed to meet it. Not, however, until his "hour" arrived. He seemed to be working on a schedule—so little time, and so much to do. But when his "hour" came, he was ready.

Even the strongest, whitest, sweetest soul the earth has known was not exempt from suffering, agony, and death. He did not talk about justice; he did not expect it; he did not receive it. He talked only of love.

Why should there be so much suffering in life? Why has the world been crucified twice on the cross of war in one generation? Nobody knows or can guess. Yet it is the major fact of life faith has to do with.

We, each of us, have a sense of wrongness, of insufficiency, and may feel that we in some degree deserve to suffer, if only to be made purer and finer. But it was not so of Jesus, who did good, only good, always, to everybody.

Did Lincoln deserve to suffer as he did, pacing up and down the White House at the news of great slaughter? Yet would he have been Lincoln if he had not felt woe at the mutilation of his people—and our people?

No, there is something else in life beside suffering for sin, our sin or the sin of others. There is an undeserved suffering —the problem of the book of Job and the life of Jesus— which opens another door of truth.

It is this unmerited suffering which more than anything else purifies and exalts the human soul. If we suffer for our wrongdoing or by it, we pay a penalty; if we meet undeserved suffering, it is something extra.

A famous lawyer who suffered excruciating pain for years, for no reason apparently, said to me, "By mastering pain, I feel that I have created something of value in myself, and perhaps in the universe."

Yes, each one has his cross to bear, a light cross indeed alongside the mighty cross of Jesus, but it means much to know that we do not walk alone along a shadowy way, that we are not picked out for punishment.

Also, it should teach us that there is a vast sympathy, understanding, and hope in the scheme of things, which takes account of our suffering, and if we bear it bravely and faithfully, will not let it be lost.

After all, what is our little suffering, keen though it be, compared to the vast sorrow of Jesus, in whose black mantle our little woes are lost beyond finding. In the world today suffering is so great as to be staggering.

Our little crosses have their day and cease to be, but that high, triumphant cross outside the city gate, etched against the skyline, stands as a signal and beacon for all our suffering race, that we not lose faith and hope.

THE WISDOM OF UNDERSTANDING

"There came wise men from the east." Matt. 2:1

THE ADVENT of the wise men asking about the crib of Christ adds a touch of strangeness and wonder to the record —how men of science came in quest of a newborn truth they had never found.

The shepherds saw no star. The wise men heard no angelic anthem. Each followed his own leading. Simple watchers of sheep and stately stargazers found the same truth. It is middle-class minds that boggle things. The wise men followed such light as they had, a pilgrim star. They were old men who refused to give up and let life trample them down. No doubt their neighbors thought they were crazy, but they had adventure in their hearts.

Therein they were wise. When we let that spark die in us, we are done. They offered their most precious gifts to a Child of another race, another land. Humility is the beginning, if not the end, of all high wisdom.

Who is wise? What is wisdom? In the wisdom books of the Bible are many tributes to this rare quality, more valuable than gems, more priceless than all the gold in all the hills. To get understanding is the real business of living.

But what is understanding? It is to see beneath the surface, to find that which stands under things, supports and sustains them. It goes down to the foundations of things and learns not only what but why they are.

All of us see the things people do, but the wise man seeks "the moving why they do it." He wants to know not merely what people are, but how they got that way. Such insight makes for understanding, for charity, for kindness.

The only wise man, Socrates said, is the man who knows how little he knows. Other men are ignorant but do not know it. Then he added, "At least I have learned that I do not know." After all, how little we really know.

Our knowledge, about which we boast, is a tiny, glimmering spark of light in a vast unfathomable darkness. The more we learn, the deeper the mystery around us. But if we are wise, we know what mystery is the shadow of truth.

The older one grows, the less one knows and the more profound is his trust, if he is wise. Science knows how things can be used. It does not know what anything is. Edison used electricity, but he did not know what it was.

No one knows what life is. It just is, as mysterious in its essence as in its origin. It is a kind of energy which has a mind of its own. Tennyson said that if we could know how a flower grows, we could know what God is.

"Consider the lilies, how they grow," said Jesus. We ponder the mystery of the lily, we wonder at its beauty, but we do not know how it grows—why it is white, and the violet blue, and the rose red.

What directs the migration of birds? What kind of a compass does a homing pigeon carry in his mind? What is instinct? What fills the interstellar space? Just emptiness? Look at a snowflake under a microscope; did ever a poet imagine such exquisite geometry?

A wise man has and keeps a grand curiosity in his heart; he is not satisfied with glib answers to great questions. He thinks, seeks, and tries to dig into the nature of things. Wonder, if it is wise, becomes humble of heart.

Wisdom is more than cunning, more than astuteness, more than knowledge. Lincoln was cunning in the way he handled his cabinet, each of whom thought himself greater than the president.

A cunning man can get things for himself, a temporary gain, often at the cost of a permanent injury. An astute man can get the better of a horse trade. But in the end he may defeat himself, if he is merely clever, and nothing else.

If Lincoln had been merely cunning and astute, he would have been a good politician, as indeed he was, but not a statesman. All his cunning was used not for himself, but toward one aim and goal—to save the Union.

He could not be swerved from that long-range purpose—no offer of office, no threat, no cleverness in others could turn him aside. In the midst of all complications and compromises he kept a straight course to his goal.

He was a wise man from the West, undismayed by disaster, undaunted by ridicule and the pettiness of men. Seeking to conciliate both sides, he seemed to both to be uncertain, hesitating, vacillating. But he was none of these things.

"With malice toward none, with charity for all," he did his work, and ascended in a chariot of tragedy at a time when he was most needed. How desperately the world needs such men—not smart sophisticates whose wisdom is not wise.

Our wisecracks are brittle and break. If our wisdom is truly wise, it does not crack. We are smitten with the curse of cleverness; it is vivacious, shallow, empty. We want men who have the wisdom of faith, of hope, of love.

Mayhap in the end wise men of the East and wise men of the West will meet, and there will be a finer wisdom than ever the world has known.

THE IMMORTAL FAITH

"He is not here, but is risen." Luke 24:6

THAT A day in spring should be set aside to celebrate the returning tide of life and the spirit of Jesus is in accord with the fitness of things, as if the seasons of the soul were in accord with the seasons of the year.

It is more than beautiful; it unites faith with life, linking the fresh buds of renewed spring with the ancient poetries and pieties of the human heart. So run the records of all time as far back as records go.

Many folks have left no written records of their history, only monuments of their immortal faith in the immortal life. It is strange beyond words—man meets death, defies it, and by faith transcends its dark shadow.

Such a faith itself, deep in the soul of man, is a mighty fact. Where did he get it? What sustains it in the forlorn march of dust unto dust? Is is vanity, or is there something deeper than we have yet fathomed?

Why should man, of all the creatures on the earth, refuse to let death have the last word, and assert that he has something within him which soars, sees, and sings? Nothing on earth is more astonishing.

Yet it is in harmony with the deepest fact of nature. In nature there is no death; there is only living and living again —death is the thing that makes for life. Without death there would be no life.

Nothing in nature dies or is lost, but only changes its form and lives again. In nature death is the miry road back to life, and only by dying daily do we live at all. In Jesus was life, so intense that it became light.

To think of such a personality going out like a candle does not make sense. His life and death changed the meaning of life and death for all. The old wheel of life was broken, and the human soul was at last set free.

Before he came, the future life brought no joy, only weariness and endless transmigrations, or a pale shadow of this life in classic poetry. He lifted it up, made it a city of God, where there is light and hope and joy.

As a mere animal, a victim of time and not of eternity, man, however clever, is ridiculous. He is overprovisioned for so short a journey; his outfit of powers and possibilities is out of all proportion to his short life.

In other words, if this life is all, why these extra mental and moral powers which set him apart from the animal? Why should he be required to obey eternal moral law if his life is but for a day? Why these strange thoughts that wander through eternity, if man is here today and gone tomorrow?

Why should he not be content, for the sake of survival, with the swiftness of the deer, the strength of the lion, the vision of the eagle? Here is a basic lack of adjustment, a being fitted to live one life and made to lead another.

Those who take as "proof" only what is shown by precision methods had better take another look. Every day we live by things we know more certainly than we know anything in a laboratory or a court of law.

The materialist, once so confident, is in a bad way these days. The "matter" of which he was so sure has gone out from under him. He is left up in the air and cannot make up in techniques what is lacking in tissue.

The whole situation has changed, and it may change again. Easter comes not with arguments, but with anthems—telling its story of new life and hope beyond our dreams, for all the silent people we call the dead.

At the moment the world is tired, old, frightened; its mood is unhappy. We are actually anxious about the survival of the race and the existence of civilization. But that mood will pass, and the shadow of fear will lift.

Of course every man sheds his illusions; but we never quite shed our discontent of having shed them, and it is "a divine discontent." Just so we seem to lose our faith, but if we are wise, it will come back stronger—as a trust.

Such at least has been my experience, and the older I grow, the more confident I am of "the ultimate decency of things and the wise kindness of the veiled Father of men," whose thoughts and ways are above our little minds.

This too I know, as I know nothing else, that without a growing and glowing faith in the immortal life, our little life ebbs out its brief day of futility. Nothing takes the heart out of life like loss of faith in its value.

To think cheaply of ourselves and our fellows, to regard human beings as talking animals, is to undermine the highest and best life. This sort of thing is in the air; current books are full of it.

No, thank God, there is something in the human heart which defies dull death in behalf of things that make it worth our time to live, something we must not let die, or even grow dim, else we lose our way in the dark.

Said Emerson that it is man who makes truth great, not truth that makes man great. Both statements are true. "He is not here, but is risen."

BRAVE SOULS HIDE SORROW

"And he washed his face, and went out." Gen. 43:31

THESE WORDS are from the story of Joseph and his brethren. First they had tried to kill him through jealousy. Then they sold him into slavery in Egypt. But he became the chief minister of the king.

In the meantime—and it had been a mean time—famine had driven his family to seek food in Egypt, where the river Nile never failed to make its valley a garden, when the more arid land of his father was bare. The brothers did not recognize Joseph in his high office. He knew them, yet he dared not make himself known to them. In private his heart was aching, and he wept bitter tears of sorrow and pity.

But "he washed his face, and went out," hiding his love and sorrow. Not until later, when he was ready—having tested them betimes—did he reveal himself to them; and the group of brothers wept for joy.

How much hidden sorrow, how much secret grief there is all around us, often behind bright, smiling faces. Sometimes out of pride, sometimes for other reasons, people conceal the bitter hurts and horrors of life.

There is a skeleton in every closet, tucked away from prying eyes. Often our laughter keeps its rattle from being heard. The valiant way in which people bear in silence wounds which make their hearts ache!

One thinks of the king of Israel when his city was besieged and his people were starving. He walked the wall of the city wearing his royal robes.

Aghast at what he heard, the king rent his robe, and the people saw, to their horror, that he wore a suit of sackcloth underneath, next to his skin. No one guessed or even imagined his hidden agony for his people.

Outwardly he was calm; inwardly he was distracted, humble-minded, burdened by the common woe and by a sense of his unworthiness. Just so, often Lincoln told a joke to keep his own heart from breaking under the strain of woes when our country was torn asunder and struggling in the death grip of war.

No wonder he said, "I was driven to my knees because there was nowhere else to go"—he who knew his own helplessness, and learned in prayer the helpfulness of God. Behind his endless jokes lay a profound sorrow.

When William of Orange died, they found on his breast a plain gold locket containing a lock of hair, the hair of his wife, much loved and long dead. Such little tokens reveal what a man is, his hidden love and grief.

Years ago, while crossing the Atlantic on a steamer, I read a story. The title eludes my memory, but the last scene remains in my heart. It told of a girl of highborn origin who fell into hard lot. At the last she was in a cab, all crumpled up, going to Victoria Station in London with money enough only to pay her fare and buy a cup of tea. Yet when she left the cab, she walked away as proudly as if she had been a queen.

Blood does tell—and grit and pluck and grace. Some people squeak and go under; others face up and keep up. They meet disaster with poise, patience, with sheer fortitude and courage.

Such people do us no end of good by their valor. Like the woman to whom a surgeon whispered the word "malignant" in reference to her husband. The word staggered her, yet I saw her pull herself together and meet the blow.

It was magnificent. Stunned by a word softly spoken, and no wonder, she met it with high heroism, even when her heart was broken. She found in her own soul and in God that which enabled her to face the worst that life could do.

"Then I came to them of the captivity, . . . that dwelt by the river of Chebar, and I sat where they sat, and remained there astonished," wrote the prophet Ezekiel. But we do not always see what another man sees—gallantly he hides it from us.

"Thou art unto them as a very lovely song," was said of Ezekiel, he who entered into the sorrow of others, and helped to heal it by his sympathy and understanding. He saw through the veil to the badge of mourning behind.

Daily I see dimly the heavy burdens people bear, the sorrows they meet, the hardships they endure, the handicaps they confront, and I remain astonished beyond words at their unsung dignity.

For the rest, if we meet sorrow, let us bear it without letting it cast its shadow over others. If we face danger, let us dare it and defy it. If we find happiness, let us share it, not hoard it, and so double its joy. Whatever may befall, we can do our best, be our best, seek and find the best in others, knowing that "this too shall pass away," leaving in our hearts a deposit of kindness and the strength to lend a hand to another in his need.

Aye, we can be "a little kinder than necessary," the while we trust the veiled kindness of the Father of all, who knows and sustains us.

MEASURING LIFE

"A man's life consisteth not . . . of things." Luke 12:15

How SHALL we measure life? By what rule shall we gauge our years, whether we are living, or only partly living, or just passing the time?

Shall we measure life by its length? Shall we say that he who lives longest lives best? Few would say so, though all of us wish to live long enough to carry out some plan, and to see, if only in part, the fruits of our labor.

Yet it is possible for a man who has lived long to have lived too little. No, time is not the true test. Keats, Burns, Byron died early, yet they lived richly. Upon Jesus, the greatest of all lives, night fell before noon.

The size of the canvas does not decide the value of a painting. Nor does the number of our years determine the worth of our life. Time teaches wisdom, if we have ears to hear; it softens sorrows and subdues passions. But it may also wear us down, and bring us to a set, gray, apathetic end.

It is not how long we live, many years or few, that counts, but how deeply, how creatively. Our little span of years is as nothing in the long sweep of time. Our life is as a tale that is told, a mist that melts—and we are gone.

Shall we measure life by things? Is that man to be reckoned as having lived most who has accumulated the most property? Few of us would think so, though most of us live as if we thought so. A rich man may live richly, but so can a poor man, in the goods we call wealth. Things do not make or unmake life.

The names that shine brightest in the crown of the race are men and women, almost all of them, who cared nothing for money. Jesus had no money, or very little. Francis of Assisi wedded Lady Poverty, and went singing through the world, if only to show how rich life can be without the things we think are needed to live.

A wise man sees things at their proper value, as a means to an end. He knows, too, how many things there are in the world for which he has not use, how many things he can get along without; he does not require much to be happy.

How Much Land Does a Man Need? is the title of a famous Tolstoi story. The man wanted all the land in sight, and still more and more. At the end they took a spade, dug a hole, made it just long enough—seven feet—and buried him. He had collapsed grasping for land, but a grave was all that he needed at the last.

If neither time nor wealth is the true test of life, what is its real measure? Happiness? But what is happiness, and who are the happy? Is it contentment, ease of mind? Then, as a rule, only meager, unimaginative, vegetative souls are happy. Are we quite willing to admit that this is true?

Souls tuned to a higher pitch, vivid, vibrant, sensitive, torn by revolt against wrong and ugliness, shot through with fury and despair, are seldom happy. Yet to such souls the race owes its soul, not to the stupid and unfeeling who live like a cow chewing her cud, untroubled by a spark. Agony is better than inertia!

Was Jeremiah happy, or Dante, or Lincoln? Do they not show us that there is no visible tie between magnificent living and happiness? Besides, who that seeks happiness ever finds it? Happiness comes a surprise, if at all, when we are busy about something else more important.

If not happiness, can we say that success is the measure of life? Then it is men of low aims that are victors in life, commonplace souls who have no soaring vision to lure and lead them. By this test a man who links his life with something too great to be realized in his lifetime is a failure. Did not Browning teach us once and for all that low-vaulted ideals are the real failures?

If by success we mean not petty gains near by, but some grand design for human freedom and fellowship, and daring adventure in its behalf, giving our lives for a goal our earthly eyes will never see, then the success which men call failure is almost the measure of life. But not as the world reckons success.

What, then, is the real measure of life—your life and mine? What can it be but growth of mind and soul, the building of our little lives into a plan or purpose greater than ourselves, the making of a beloved community?

The soul of all improvement is the greatest improvement of the soul, said Socrates ages ago. How much have we grown since yesteryear? Do we see beauty where we did not see it before, even in the mud and scum of things?

Are we gentler, kinder, more compassionate? Do we understand more profoundly?

Are we less stolid and more sympathetic? Are we striving Godward, though it is through pain and struggle, with keener perceptions, clearer judgments, and finer loyalties? Here lies the real test of our fleeting lives.

If we have sloughed off sloth, if we have dropped fear, hate, bitterness, and all self-deception, and have learned to live because we love, glad to live and unafraid to die, then we are advancing toward the measure and meaning of life.

MEMORIAL DAY

Thus saith the Lord, . . . I made covenant with your fathers."
Jer. 34:13

What is our republic? It is a contract in which three parties are involved, the dead, the living, and those yet unborn.

A nation is a historic memory, a human fraternity, a spiritual prophecy. It is more than geography, more than a business concern. It is an ideal born of insight, and the struggle and suffering shared in its behalf.

If poised in an airplane we could look down upon our whole country, what a picture would lay spread out below—mountains, lakes, rivers, cities shining in the sunlight, parklike farms dotted with homes, trains running like shuttles in a loom, temples of art and piety, and the graves of our dead.

But that is not the nation; it is only the scene and setting of its drama. He who would see the nation must have eyes to behold the march of ideas, the growth and flowering of principles, the unfolding of laws, the network of reverences, hopes, dreams, the mystic ties of memory uniting past, present, and future.

All that our fathers brought with them to these shores; all that has been achieved in our struggle for the advance of mankind; all the moral causes and spiritual attachments which move the hearts of our people—these, fused together into a living unity, make the reality and sanctity of the nation.

How fitting, then, that we have a patriotic sabbath, a sacrament of memory, in honor of our republic, and in gratitude for all who have served its ideal and its faith, all who have fallen on red fields of war that it might grow and be glorified, that liberty, justice, and good will may live and abide.

Born of battle years, it is a day of peace, rich in pathos and breathing the spirit of gentleness. As the flags are run up, and the flowers are strewn upon the graves of the dead, there is no thought of strife, but of tender seriousness, of kindliness, of reverent and consecrating memory.

Every year this day returns with added sanctity and suggestion, as war is added to war in the sad and tragic annals of the race, with new graves to decorate, with deepening thoughts of a precious and heroic heritage.

> That which our fathers wrought
> With high prophetic thought
> Must be defended.

Surely he is a poor prophet, and no poet at all, who does not see the hand of God in the founding of our republic. Truly God made a covenant with our fathers when they brought forth "a new nation" in a new world, dedicated to the liberty, the equality, the high-hearted hopes of human beings.

Of what were those men thinking who gave us the Declaration of Independence and the Constitution? What were the hopes and dreams and aspirations of those mighty souls of an elder time? Today, amid chaos and alien isms, it behooves us to read anew the history of our beginnings that the fire of faith may be kindled again.

Led by Washington, our fathers kept the covenant at Bunker Hill and Valley Forge and Yorktown, as later Lincoln kept his contract with Washington at Shiloh and Gettysburg and Cold Harbor and the Wilderness.

Those great souls kept their contract with us who live in a new and strange time. Looking forward, they saw a vast nation, of many races and tongues, united and free, giving shape and leadership to the history of the world.

God be thanked, we kept our contract with them in an hour dark with destiny, when the foulest slavery that ever crawled across the earth threatened to engulf the whole race and drag it down to some subhuman level. We did not falter, we did not fail, we did not betray the sacred legacy of our fathers!

Fidelity to all that is holy in our history requires "that we here highly resolve" to keep inviolate our contract with the dead, and with those yet unborn. Nor fear nor greed nor time-serving must turn us aside, or make us forget.

If our republic fails, it will be because we are false to the faith of our fathers. Our task is to show that folk of many races can live together without rancor, and many creeds without feud, and that working in fellowship, we can create a social order that is just and free and wise, with hope for all.

To this task and dream let us dedicate ourselves anew on this day of memory, when we bow in honor of all who fell at home, and in the far places of the earth, and on the gray solitudes of the sea, that the United States may live and serve.

My life, every life, is but one note in a symphony, the end of which we may never know, one word in a sentence, the last syllable of which we may never hear; but no one lives in vain who helps to make a better world for those who follow him—a gentler path for little feet to walk in days ahead.

HOPE UNDEFEATED

"Behold, I make all things new." Rev. 21:5

Truly, "hope springs eternal in the human breast," as the poet Pope tells us. Perhaps the greatest fact about man is his unconquerable hopefulness.

Often defeated, long delayed, and still unfulfilled, yet hope lives in the human heart. Like a taper in the wind, at times it burns low and sputters, but it never quite goes out. For when hope dies, man is dead.

At Advent we recall the heroic and thrilling hope in the hearts of the people of the Bible, forefelt in the Old Testament, fulfilled in the New Testament. Like an arch of promise it spanned the ages, becoming more spiritual and luminous. It saw a daystar in the bosom of midnight, and followed it.

The last book of the Old Testament closes with a faint hope and a dark threat, to be followed by four hundred years of tragic history. The world was changed beyond belief. There were times when the earth seemed swept clean of every divine footprint. Yet incredibly that mighty hope survived.

Back of that hope burned a tenacious, unshakable faith in God. That which is not based upon justice must perish; God has revealed justice to his people; humanity exists to realize justice; justice will be realized at last—such was the creed of the prophets, from the days of Amos on.

It was magnificent! Those sons of the twilight lived expectantly, despite all inertia and apostasies. They lived with the future in their hearts, eager, forward looking. If at times they were unhopeful, they were never hopeless, and their flaming speech was free from the poison of despair.

"Hope deferred maketh the heart sick," wrote the author of Proverbs, but the prophets stood by the covenant God had made with his people. They refused to think, even in their darkest hours, that God would allow the human soul to be betrayed and mocked by its own purest and holiest visions. They foresaw a higher type of man.

What great words are these, "Tribulation worketh patience; and patience, experience; and experience, hope." Without faith in God, alas, it is often the other way around —experience of life makes men hopeless. It shakes the stars out of their eyes, leaving them to fight a dim battle in the doubtful land.

Watts was wrong when in his great painting "Hope" he drew a young woman, sitting on a globe, under a sky full of stars, holding a harp in her hand. Every string of the harp, but one, is broken, and she is about to strike the last string. She should have been an old woman, her face engraved by experience, her hands blue-veined, strong, gentle—the ripe, rich hope of age.

How stands the case with us today? A thousand years of history swept swiftly over the world between 1914 and 1945, leaving a wreckage of broken dreams and blasted hopes. Instead of great dreams coming true, we saw cruelty and chaos unimaginable, two ghastly wars, and horror upon horror!

No wonder we are disillusioned, frustrated, bewildered, tired, tempted to yield to the cynicism which whispers that man is the dupe of some divine delusion, a pawn of fate, or worse still, a toy of blind chance. Such a mood is understandable, but it is also unthinkable—it would be the final treachery against both God and man, proof positive of collaboration with the devil, a subversive influence too black to tolerate and too bleak to endure.

Alexander Pope's wit is too easy, "Blessed is he who expects nothing, for he shall never be disappointed." Wiser by far is the other beatitude, so deeply engraved in the annals of faith, "Expect great things from God; attempt great things for God." Nothing can ultimately defeat such an active faith.

Emerson went about peeping into every cradle, looking for a Messiah—therein he was wise. Of old there came a Baby, "one of the children of the year," whose life of heroic moral loveliness gave a new date to time, and a new depth and wonder to human life. The manger-cradle refuted despair.

Someone ought to write a book *The Fifty Decisive Babies of the World.* It would be a radiant research, disproving old cynicisms and pessimisms. In a world wistful with half revelations we keep vigil in our hearts, waiting for the coming of the sons of God, those "large, eternal fellows" born to victory.

Always there is a sense of Something very near, trying to lay hands upon us; Something seeking to make itself seen and heard and felt. The world aches with the urgency of a Silence that tries to speak, but it is tongue-tied because we do not listen and hear and obey.

Here and there a hint, a gleam of the Eternal breaks through, and as much or as little as we see is our religion now and then; in the face of the very young or the very old, we see a flash of a face, veiled in beauty, yet coming nearer—the face of the future man, gentle, just, heroic, happy, and free!

"Behold, I make all things new," a new man in a new world.

WHY WASTE TIME IN WORRYING?

"Take therefore no thought for the morrow: for the morrow shall take thought for the things of itself."
Matt. 6:34

MAN IS born to worry, as the sparks fly upward. If he has nothing to worry about, he manufactures hobgoblins to keep in practice. Really, he does not want to be rid of worry; it seems to make him happy.

Many years ago a dear woman, eighty-five years of age, taught me two lessons which have helped me greatly. She learned them by living, not without difficulty, and she thought they had added years to her life, as well as life to her years.

First, we must learn to forgive people for what they are, as well as for what they do. What they do grows out of what they are—they may not know it, they may not be able to help it. We cannot make people over.

No doubt we would like to make them over—as the old button maker wanted Peer Gynt ground up and made over. Even our friends may wish that they could make us over, in some parts at least; but they cannot do it.

If a man has no money sense, we cannot give him any. If he lacks a sense of time, we cannot impart it to him. In any case, if we could make people over, we might make matters worse—better leave matters as they are.

Second, never worry about a thing until it happens. It may

never happen and we waste a lot of good worry. Once in a blue moon the thing we worry about does happen, but other things happen, too, changing the setting and the scene.

Seldom does anything happen as we see it when we pop awake at night in a cold sweat of fear, and our imagination puts on a moving picture of the horror, and we have to see it over and over again until we are worn out.

If we wait until a thing happens, at least we are worrying about a reality, not about a mere figment of the fancy. We can see it, take its measure, and handle it. Whereas if it is imaginary, it eludes our grasp.

Worry is interest paid in advance, which is not good business; if the thing does not happen, it is a dead loss. It spoils tomorrow before tomorrow arrives, makes us tired before the day begins: "The morrow shall take thought for the things of itself."

But something will happen. Now and then it's something we never thought about. Edwin Booth, one of our greatest actors, was a noble Christian spirit. But he fell into the bad habit of worrying about everything.

Then suddenly something happened, worse than anything he had ever dreamed in his worst nightmare. His brother shot President Lincoln! He was stunned, stupefied; he never again played in Washington; he could not.

The shadow lay upon his life like a pall to the end, greater than any tragedy he had ever played on the stage. Whether it healed him of worrying about little things or not, there is no record. He went, a wounded spirit, to his grave.

How can we deal with worry? For one thing, we must learn to think with our minds, not with our emotions, least of all with our imaginations. Emotional control is a fine art, easier to master for some than for others.

If we calmly line up the things we are worrying about, one by one, and look at them in the daylight, we can see what a shabby lot they are. We can see their size and shape, and how futile it is to bother about them.

Worry, of course, is a form of fear, a slow poison which filters into our souls. We may not admit that we are afraid, but we are. When we take a straight look at the things that frighten us, we must surely see how harmless they are.

A simple religious faith is the best protection against both fear and worry. It arms us against evil, real or imaginary; it puts our affairs into hands other than our own. We may have concern, but no wearying, fruitless worry.

Faith will stop worry when it starts, so it will not stick in the mind like a bur and sting like a bee. It is an inside job, and by trust in God, and a wise handling of our minds, we can do it and be rid of nagging worry.

The wisdom of Solomon failed to cure him of "fears in the night"; but faith in God does not fail if we know how to use it. Our little worries have their day and pass away, but life ought not to be marred by them.

HOW TO LIVE

"Jesus said . . . ." John 21:23

How to live is one matter. Jesus came, he said, to show us what God is, what life is, and how to live it, making it not a job, but a joy.

As we listen to his words, it almost takes our breath away. He was so wise that he was simple, and so simple that he was wise. He taught in parables and pictures, dipping his truth in all the colors of life.

As we listen, God is near and very real, walking our human way. Now he is a farmer sowing seed, now a father with two wayward sons, now a shepherd seeking a lost sheep, now a fisherman casting his net, now an employer of labor listening to complaints about hours and wages.

That is what God is like, said Jesus. Trust him, talk to him as your father; he is not far off up in the sky, but nearer than your own soul. Live with him, put all your treasure in his bank—it will not fail. Seek life, not merely a living, life for everybody; seek truth, justice, beauty, love.

Seek the kingdom of God and his goodness; if we seek first things first, all the rest will be added. There will be bread enough and to spare, not only bread, but beauty, kindness, good will, a heart to feel and a hand to help; life every way will be rich, and death but a passing shadow.

No wonder "the common people heard him gladly," as much for what he said as for the way he said it. Yet they were amazed at his words, even as we are, because we have missed the point of life, and put the cart before the horse. If Jesus was right, our fear and fret and wasting worry are wrong and futile.

A great teacher, some say, but awfully impractical; we look at him with wistful eyes, wishing that what he tells us might be true. But does our way work, wearing us to a frazzle with fear and fret? If the way of Jesus is difficult, is not our way a weariness, bankrupt, and a failure?

Really, are we practical folk, with our single-minded pursuit of personal gain, letting the other man hustle for himself? On that basis is the world a success, when hunger stalks the earth, and old wars give place to rumors of new wars? Is there any dining car on our human train?

Some of the words of Jesus, we agree, are right down-to-earth plain sense. About loving our neighbor, for example, since anyone can see that the alternative is first fear, then fighting, or else freezing indifference.

Only, like the man in the parable, we want to select our neighbor, but Jesus will not have it so. Our neighbor, he said, is the man who needs us, whatever his race or color or creed may be. And that makes a difficulty.

Of course we cannot be fond of everybody; the human heart is limited. No one can feel for a stranger as he does for a friend. But to love a person in the true sense is sincerely to desire his highest good, and we dare not do anything else for anyone, not even with our enemy—or we destroy ourselves.

Jesus said that to hold hates and grudges, to refuse to forgive, is to refuse forgiveness for ourselves—leaving ourselves out in the cold. To live, then, we must forgive; that is, give back love, if we would have it given to us. The Golden Rule applies here, as everywhere else in life.

Also, Jesus did not teach such a principle as the Golden Rule and leave it at that. Fine phrases were not enough; he acted upon his truth, proving it not merely by words but by deeds. And he promised that if we do likewise, we shall know many things now dim—because we know as much as we do, and no more.

If we had never read the words of Jesus, and heard them for the first time today, they would startle us, stun us, and stir us as no other words ever did. Something would take place deep down in us, a shift of interest, a new focus of life. We would see that we are seeking the wrong things, following false goals—off the beam in our thinking and living.

No wonder we are all tied up with fears, anxieties, and forebodings. We could be free of all these things if we kept in the way that Jesus taught. Jesus had no fear, and having no fear, he knew no hate—and where fear ends, life begins, life that is happy and free. No wonder the very thought of Jesus makes us wistful, wishing for the courage and the humility to do what he tells us.

After all, life is all we have. If we cannot find meaning in its mystery, if we cannot make music of its discords, there is nothing else for us. It is soon over and done and gone, and we have not lived, or have only partly lived. Jesus knew how to live, and he can teach us the art; it is wise to give him a try.

What did Jesus get out of life? A muddy death at last on a dark cross outside the city gate, amid hissing hate and howling anger? He got nothing but life—an empty tomb, and a luminous trail for us to follow, if we would know what life is, and how it can soar beyond what we call death.

TELLING THE TRUTH

"Speaking the truth in love." Eph. 4:15

OF COURSE we ought to tell the truth, but it is not easy to obey both halves of this text. Sometimes we tell the truth because it hurts; more often we withhold the truth out of kindness.

"Truth is such a rare thing, it is delightful to tell it," said Emily Dickinson. Truth is rare; it is hard to know and difficult to tell, even when we want to tell it and try to tell it.

Someone said there are two ways to deal with the truth—tell it or hide it. No, there are three ways—tell it twice as big as it is, half as big as it is, or just as big as it is.

In court we take an oath, or a vow, to tell the truth, the whole truth, and nothing but the truth. How can we do it unless we see clearly, know the facts, and choose our words and our tone of voice?

Our silences, too, need careful watching. One can express, suggest, or suppress the truth without saying a word. An expression of face, a shrug of the shoulders, the lifting of an eyebrow, a pause, a gesture—and a tale can be twisted out of all semblance to the truth.

A slight inflection of the voice can turn a truth into a lie, conveying a totally different impression, altering the atmosphere. No wonder the Bible tells us that we shall be judged by every idle, as well as evil, word. How often the old book bids us watch and rule our tongues!

No wonder, too, that Jesus said that anything beyond Yea, yea, and Nay, nay, "cometh of evil." But such verbal self-denial, such severe rationing of speech is too much for us, since we must always be talking, whether we have anything to say or not, whether what we say is true or not.

Nine tenths of our talk is useless, but not harmful—it is not meant to hurt. It is just talk for the sake of talk, for fun and foolishness. We may stretch a fish story with no intent to deceive—it is just an exercise of the imagination. But there is something more than this.

It is amazing how much shabby, second-hand lying all of us do, unless we have a care—lying through laziness. We hear a yarn about someone, and pass it along, without taking time and pains to verify it.

As gossip, it severs friendships; as bigotry, it makes for bitterness; as propaganda, it is poison. A little thought, a little care would have convinced us of its error. It grows as it goes, since people love to tell evil tidings; and before we know it, it is a hateful thing.

How much dirty, ugly talk slops about in the gutter *sub rosa* because we respectable liars have neither the industry to check up on our chatter nor the kindness to remain silent until we do. It would horrify us to be called deliberate liars, but we do not tell the truth.

Such muddleheadedness makes bad blood in politics, in religion, in race relations. It sets up barriers, because people otherwise intelligent, even kind, talk rubbish through culpable ignorance or sinful carelessness in dealing with others.

It is plain enough that the spirit of honor, respect, service, good will between man and man, mind and mind—the spirit we call love—is the only possible and essential spirit in which to talk about anybody. "The truth of truths is love," as the poet Philip James Bailey tells us.

Still, we are only at the beginning of the matter. If we are to tell the truth, we must first know the truth, and that is not easy. To know the truth is as much an obligation of honor as to speak it, but more of us seem to be more careful about the second than about the first.

To know the truth, to tell the truth, we must be the truth; these three, and the greatest of these is to be the truth. To do it to perfection is the finest of arts, and few attain it. Yet nothing less is required of us—let us be sure of that.

Each of us lives in two worlds. The inner world of ideas, dreams, memories, hopes, fears, faiths, regrets. Then there is the outer world, the stage on which we act our part, where we strut, fret, work, suffer, win, fail, live, and die. To be true means that these two worlds must fit together.

This is what is meant by that purity of heart by which men come to see God. Alas, how far we are from it. This is a nobler thing than telling the truth, nobler even than knowing the truth, because it includes them both. Who is there among us who has come near to it?

"I am . . . the truth," said a sweet voice long ago; the truth that makes all other truth true. Most of us are as yet, to some extent, living lies. God help us to speak the truth, to know the truth, to be the truth.

LIVING BY THE DEEP SPRINGS OF LIFE

"So teach us to number our days." Ps. 90:12

It is possible to be happy in an unhappy world without being hard of heart. We cannot control what happens to us betimes, but we can decide what it will do to us. We can have happiness in what happens to us, in what we do with life.

Indeed, we cannot do much to help an unhappy world if we are bowed down by its weight of woe. In days like these it is vital that we fortify our hearts against the fears and terrors that infest the earth.

About twenty years ago a wise man remarked that "the scare has superseded the vision as the moving force in life." Since then the "scare" has become a horror which dominates our thoughts and acts and plans. Here is where our religion ought to help us, if we know how to use it.

Time adds years to our life; religion ought to add life to our years. Faith is the one force that can meet defeat, and even despair, and not be defeated, much less give up hope. The secret of life is to be ruled not by our fears, but by the faiths that drive out fears as so many imps.

Few of us can be satisfied with the way we live. Let us try again and see if we cannot do a better job of living, put more into life, get more out of it. For life is all we have. If we do not learn to live, it will be over and done and gone before we know it.

"Buy up the time," said a wise saint; get a corner on it, use every bit of it without waste. It is amazing the time we fritter away, killing it instead of filling it, whereas we ought to learn how to turn time into life. Else time eats up life, and we merely live to pass the time.

To that end we must learn to live by the deep springs of life, not by its transient emotions. Rain water splashes the street and makes it dirty and slippery, but it is soon gone and forgotten. The abiding sentiments of love and loyalty remain, and these tell us the truth about life.

John Morley, in trying to explain the mystery of Gladstone, said that "he lived from deeper depths and stood on tiptoe to the future." No wonder that at eighty-nine he was as fresh as a spring morning, and wrote the secret of it to his children, "Put habit on the side of the inner life."

One can do so many new things to drink from the deep springs of life: alter old attitudes, adopt new habits of mind and heart, throw out old grudges, forget old blunders, and make a new start. Let us make some vows and keep them, and the first should be to exemplify a spirit of respect, good will, and understanding toward folk of all races, all faiths, all colors, at all cost.

Why should our first feeling about a man of another race be one of indifference or suspicion? He is a human being, with feelings like our own. Why indulge the vanity that we are somehow superior, and have some rights that do not belong to him? Let us learn to honor the human, as human.

Also, by the mercy of God, let us have the good sense and

good faith to attribute to those who differ from us in religion—those who use other forms and symbols—the same degree of sincerity that we claim for ourselves. In our religion at least we ought to be fair and kind. Is that asking too much?

Let us have nothing to do with anyone who is spreading anti-Semitism, anti-Catholicism, or anti-Protestantism, or any other antiattitude evil, ugly, and unkind. Instead, let us seek to cultivate comradeship with all who seek to exalt love and good fellowship in the world.

In short, let us here highly resolve to live and let live, to think and let think, aye, to live and help live, since each has a hard fight against many odds. If we appreciate a little more and criticize a little less, guided by our admirations rather than our disgusts, it will make life happier for all.

In the rush and hurry and tension of life today, when the whole world pours in upon us with a flood of events, it will pay richly if we form a habit of taking a little time each day to be quiet, to listen in the silence, to think about God, and pray, and get things straight on the inside.

If we make more allowance for the faults of others, and less for our own, if we are more honest with our own souls, and keep fewer shallow pretenses with which we try to deceive ourselves; if we get ourselves off our hands, and take more interest in others, the way will be clearer.

Hope much, fear not at all; do your best, seek the best in others; and trust God. If you have sorrow, bear it; if you meet danger, dare it; if you find happiness, share it. God bless us every one!

THE GREAT PRAYER

"When ye pray, say, Our Father who art in heaven."
Luke 11:2

THE DISCIPLES of Jesus, knowing his habits of devotion, followed him and heard him pray. As they listened, they realized that they did not know the alphabet of that highest of all arts.

"Lord, teach us to pray," they asked very earnestly. In response to their request Jesus gave them a little prayer which has become the best-beloved prayer on earth; "that brief, grand prayer," as Carlyle called it.

Brief it is, containing only seventy words, and grand beyond any speech other than its own; grand too in its all-inclusive and compassionate consecration, gathering up the needs and hopes of humanity.

Alas, we often use it more as an incantation than as an invocation, as if saying it were enough. Most people really pray only a few times in their lives; at other times they merely say their prayers.

The key word of the prayer is "Father," the basic truth in the life and faith of Jesus—the first word we hear from him as a child, his last word of prayer from the cross when he gave his spirit back to God.

What he meant by that word, he told us in the parable of the father, which we misname the parable of the prodigal son. The hero of that incomparable story is not the wayward son, but the old father waiting for his return, ready to forgive.

Here is the one prayer in which Hindu, Hebrew, and every kind of Christian can unite, each praying for all and all for each one. It is the model prayer for humanity and the monopoly of no one religion, no one church.

Brief, simple, profound, it is as high as the sky, as wide as the world, equal to all our mortal needs and our immortal longings. It implies democracy; it is an epitome of religions; it crystallizes theology.

"It is the politics of the kingdom of Heaven"; it gives us a faith and a philosophy of life; it tells us why we are here upon earth, what we are here to do; the truth we were meant to learn, the beauty we were sent to seek.

Nay, more, it is at once a program and a plan of action; it links our tiny will with an eternal good will; it sets the inner life in order; it prophesies the kind of society in which all souls are to assemble.

It is the one perfect private prayer; it is the most complete corporate prayer. When we say "our Father," we embrace all souls, taking the whole race into the closet with us when we offer this prayer, asking nothing for ourselves which we do not ask for all our fellow men.

A few shining sentences, wet with the tears of the human race, it tells all that we know, or need to know, finding the meaning and the mystery of life in God—mystery being the shadow of truth for which we are unready.

The most private, the most public, the most practical of all prayers, it begins and ends in God, "in whose will is our peace," in "whose service is perfect freedom," our reason for being, our haven of hope, "in whose great hand we stand."

It breathes aspiration, adoration, allegiance, petition, intercession, and forgiveness. Yet it is a dangerous prayer to offer if we harbor envy or hatred in our hearts, since it asks God to make his forgiveness the measure of our own.

It asks bread for today and hope for tomorrow. It beseeches God not to lead us into temptation, or as an old Armenian version has it, "Do not let us yield to temptation," when we are terribly tried by the wiles and woes of life.

"Deliver us from evil"—let not the black facts of life break our hearts and blast our faith. Save us from the awful fear that "what we value most is at the mercy of what we value least." Make us victors over life, not victims of the carelessness of man or the callousness of nature.

This prayer invokes the kingdom of God, not beyond life and time, but here upon earth, and issues in action to that end, uniting the power of God and the energy of man in the final enterprise of life.

It knows no race, no rank, no caste, no frontier, no enemies; it brings all men, of all types and times, into unity and fellowship in God, the Father of all, who, because he is love, is known only through love.

No word need be taken from the prayer Jesus taught us to pray; no word need be added to it. As we ponder this prayer, the wonder of it gathers and grows—in it the love of God and the need of man meet.

If this tiny prayer had been made the creed of our faith,

how different its history would have been. A prayer become a creed, a creed become a prayer—it would have saved us ages of angry debate.

When we kneel to pray and stand to sing, all our little schisms are lost in a sublime symphony; we have profound unity and triumphant fellowship. One in our nature and need, we are one also in faith and hope and love.

THE BOOK OF LIFE

"Then did I eat it; and it was in my mouth as honey."
Ezek. 3:3

THUS THE prophet Ezekiel told of his call and consecration. He was granted a vision of God and his throne, and fell on his face before it.

"Son of man, stand upon thy feet, and I will speak unto thee." Not in fear, not in abject obeisance, but erect and unafraid God would speak to him. He was sent on a mission of comfort to his people in their captivity.

A little book was given him to eat, "and it was in my mouth as honey for sweetness." It is a perfect picture of the collect for Bible Sunday, which asks us to "read, mark, learn, and inwardly digest" the Bible for our strength and comfort.

As we take food into our body for nourishment, so the spirit and teaching of this book are to be taken into our minds and hearts, and made a part of our very being. It is more than memory, more than meditation; it is assimilation. It gives us the Bible faith, the Bible point of view, the Bible stability.

It is as when we learn to play a piece of music. At first we study the score, then practice it. After a while, if we try long enough, we can play it without the score, but in our minds we still see the page. Finally the score fades away, and we play it by heart, as we say. It has entered into our mind stream.

This is the truest and most vital translation of the Bible,

whatever version we use. It means that we absorb the essence of the book, like meat and bread and medicine. As a great saint said, the Bible is the musical score, and the lives of the saints are the score played out amid the facts of life.

One of the greatest powers of the mind is our capacity to take other and greater minds into our own. An old country preacher, known to me years ago, knew two books, the Bible and Shakespeare. He lived in both books and both books lived in him—no wonder there was faith and music in his preaching.

The Bible nowhere speaks of itself as a whole. The phrase "the Word of God" is never applied to anything written. No book, not all the books in the world, could contain the word of God. "In the beginning was the Word, and the Word was with God, and the Word was God"—before all worlds. It is known not by translation, but by incarnation. "The Word became flesh and dwelt among us," but Jesus wrote nothing.

The Bible is a record, deep and age-old, of the God experiences of poets, prophets, apostles who lived with him. They suffered, sinned, and were forgiven; they knew sorrow, heartache, and despair, and set down in the granitic solidity of great prose and the flaming splendor of poetry what they learned.

The Bible is a book of life. Its art is artless. It does not argue. It does not speculate. Its characters are God, man, life, the earth, and the sky. It reveals man for what he is, a mixture of deity and dirt, mysticism and meanness. It is the most idealistic and realistic of books. Its poetry is like the winds in the trees.

Here is a book of fact, not of theory, of life and death and all that lies between and beyond. It tells the story of the birth and growth of a nation, its wandering tribes, its slavery, its moral law and social order, its rise to power, its division and downfall, its captivity—what men learned from life.

The Bible grew out of a deep, rich, age-old religious experience, and if rightly used and obeyed, it will reproduce in us the kind of life which produced it, infallibly. It is infallible, too, in the old Anglo-Saxon sense of the word *in-fall-hein,* "that which will not fall down." The facts prove it.

It is a book written from above downward. Everybody, everything in the Bible is always in the presence of God, and in relation to God. The book has no rafters, no roof. It is open to the infinite; it finds us, as Coleridge said, searching us, dividing the marrow from the bone. It has been tested by ages of living.

Not only does the Bible tell us that men learned of God in days of old; it tells us how they learned. God spoke to man in olden times, as he speaks to us, in the facts, events, actions, and persons in the drama of history, as well as in the secret places of the heart where men sought to know his will.

When the Assyrian army started west, the prophets asked what God meant by such a clash and overturning of nations. If you have read *Communism and the Conscience of the West,* by Fulton Sheen, you have heard a modern prophet asking the same question. The book shakes a man in his shoes, searching us like a flame.

Yet amid all these upheavals of history, even when the people of the Bible were carried away into a new slavery, their leaders never lost faith in God, never lost touch with him. The reality of God, the moral basis of life, the dim but growing hope of immortal life, deepened and grew; they knew no cynicism.

Then at last, after troubled tragic ages, came a voice, calm, clear, piercing, speaking "words of eternal life." A life that interprets life, answering even the unasked questions of the heart—One like ourselves, but taller of soul, taking little steps by our side to show us the way and how to go.

How can people forget or neglect this book of the life and love and law of God for our human life! It is the mother book of our literature; it is the most precious of our spiritual possessions; it is the book for the healing of human hearts, showing us the way without which there is no going. "How readest thou?"

THE MYSTERY OF MEMORY

"My times are in thy hand." Ps. 31:15

My birthday is at hand and it makes me ponder. Which birthday it is, no one need know; it is my own affair. Everyone has his secret.

The older a man grows, the less he knows and the more he wonders. The mystery deepens, and so does faith if he is wise. Even ordinary things become marvels, such as time and memory, both of which utterly baffle me.

To me time is a puzzle past finding out. The more so when to clock time we add inner time, biologic time. What time is, whether it is fact or fiction, no man truly knows.

Of course we need time to make dates, to do chores, to catch trains; and we use it without knowing what it is. A great poet thought he could hear the soft flowing of time as a river in the night, but it was only a fancy.

Why do we want to hurry into the future, faster than time is willing to take us? When I was ten, I wanted to be fifteen; when I was twenty, I wanted to be thirty. In happy moods we want time to stand still, but not for long. It is not the present, however happy, but the future that we want and long for.

Why this urge toward what is ahead of us? Some say it is a kind of instinctive sacrifice of ourselves in the interest of mankind, that we are only means to an end and must find the meaning of life in the race.

But the meaning of life is in the present moment, not in yesterday, not in tomorrow. There is no past and no future, only today. My guess is that our hunger for the future is really a hunger for eternity, not forward but upward. Is time only a measured part of that eternity in which we live now and always?

In the same way, memory is a mystery too deep to fathom. Like all mirrors, it sees everything and forgets nothing. But it is coy of its secrets. It hides much from us, else a flood of memories would wash us away.

How deep is memory; how far back does it go? No man living is just himself, alone and separate, but is the residue handed down from many ancestors. Voices from afar whisper within us; forces from long ago ripple in our blood. Our life is larger and longer than we dream.

What is instinct but organized memory? Is genius anything but memory, one wonders? Is our highest knowledge a reminiscence, as Plato taught? Is memory the mother of faith, as it is the thread on which our days are strung? So Augustine thought, as he told us on a shining page, "When I wished to find the root of my knowledge of God, I came into the great courts of memory." There he found himself, all that he had been and done, and last and greatest of all, he found God, the beginning and the end.

Will memory redeem us at last, as it has often done? "This do in remembrance of me," said Jesus. What did the psalmist mean when he wrote, "All the ends of the world shall remember and turn unto the Lord"? As if, at long last, our wayward race is to be saved by a holy, happy memory of God. Memory gives sense and sequence to our days, and is the source of more blessings than we can guess.

Hear now a story in which the mysticism of time and the mystery of memory are blended. It is a true story, as I vow, although I do not know the full meaning of it. How little we know of the meaning of our days!

In London, years ago, a dear friend and I drove to the south of England to see the village where he was born, a tiny village tucked away in a vale. In the early morning, before we started, I had a dream in which I saw a village, saw it vividly and in detail, so that I could describe it.

As we drove along the lovely countryside, I told him what I had seen in my dream—a winding road, a vine-covered church, and in the churchyard a stone so old and weather-beaten that the name on it was blurred.

"My word, old chap," my friend said in a startled tone, "here I am taking you to see my village, and you seem to have seen it in your dream. The stone you saw marks the plot where my family are buried. It is very strange."

As we entered the village, I had a sense that it was not only friendly, but in a strange way familiar, as if I had seen it and known it sometime before. It was like a home-coming—never had I felt more at home anywhere.

To this day it puzzles me beyond words. Why did I feel so instantly and utterly at home in a village I had never seen before? Nobody knows; at least I do not. Was it a memory of my soul? I wish I knew.

THE NIGHT IS ENDING

"Watchman, what of the night?" Isa. 21:11

AGAINST A dim blue sky a watchman walks the walls. "What of the night?" he is asked. "The morning cometh, and also the night," he replied.

As in nature, so in history there is a rhythm of night and day. It was too early, too dark to decide, but day follows night. Even today it is still twilight, but there are tokens of the coming day.

We have been living in one of the great night scenes of history, of which there have been many. The fall of the Roman Empire plunged the world into shadow, which deepened into the Dark Ages, lasting hundreds of years. But at last came dawn, and Europe rose "with the New Testament in her hand."

And so it will be again in our time. Always some lose heart, let go of faith, and resign themselves to the night. Contemporary prophets tell us that our country has lost faith in God, in local government, even in free enterprise. Its flame burns low, its spirit is about to sputter out.

Parleys are paralyzed, racial rancor runs rife, people turn jellyfish and want to be taken care of, the church is a failure and no one cares to attend it, materialism is supreme, the tension is so tight that our leaders die of ulcers, and over all the atom bomb—so runs the litany of despair.

Admit the facts, but do we read them aright? In spite

of "the dust of rubbled cities," and cruelties too ghastly to name, and deep dismay, belief in the possibility of a finer world emerges. A fresh wind of faith is blowing; never has man done so much for man as he is doing today in myriad ways.

Not preachers only, but men of science and historians are telling us that life does have meaning, that there is purpose in history, and that the universe should be read in moral and spiritual terms. Take three recent books by men of science: *Man Does not Stand Alone,* by A. C. Morrison; *Human Destiny,* by Lecomte du Noüy; and *What Is Life?* by Erwin Schrödinger.

The facts they recite are fantastic. Take only one. All the eels on earth assemble in the Gulf Stream off Bermuda every year to spawn. Having spawned, the old eels die. Yet every little eel goes straight as an arrow back to the river in which his mother lived. They never fail, never get lost. How do they do it? What kind of compass do they carry in their minds? Who taught them navigation? An eel is a slippery thing for an atheist to handle.

To read these books is a thrilling experience. They tell us that materialism, as we knew it in other days, is as dead as the dodo. Matter, as man thought of it, does not exist. Add the long survey of history by Arnold Toynbee, the story of civilizations long vanished, and you feel the turning of the tide of faith, flowing over the mud flats of cynicism and futility.

Has the church failed? Look at the great missionary enterprise, its far-flung frontier in many lands, and its rapid growth. In the early days of our country only one in every fifteen persons belonged to any church. In 1890, less than 23 per cent. Today one in every two people are church folk.

To be sure, as we confessed in unison at Amsterdam in 1948: "Often we have tried to serve God and mammon, put other loyalties before loyalty to Christ, confused the gospel with our own economic or national or racial interests, and feared war more than we have hated it." But we also cried out, as at Pentecost, "Men and brethren, what shall we do?"

And as at Pentecost we were told, "Repent!" that is, change our minds, or as Albert Einstein put it, "We must either change our thinking or die." A profound change is going on in the religious mind—a change from division to devotion to a common cause, from clashing creeds to clasping hands in the saving service of souls and of society. A world council of churches is now a reality.

It is a start, a step toward the discovery of the unity of the spiritual community. Also, that the physical conditions of the spiritual life must be looked after, and not be left to secular and alien isms. Never has the gospel of religion been so challenged as it is today—and a new day it is.

Yes, there are signs and gleams of a new day. The night is ending; the dawn is at hand, albeit a cloudy, confused dawn, but still a dawn. It is so in our own lives too. Let us remember, "This too will pass away." If it is night, black from pole to pole, sorrow will lift and there will be light.

God has taught us to believe that this is true of the shadow that waits for every man. It is very dark, we cannot see through its heavy draperies, but "there is light on the other side of life," as a great poet tells us, he who knew how deep, dark, and lonely life can be when death passes by.

"Watchman, what of the night? . . . The morning cometh!"

INDEX